MARTHA'S VINEYARD

A Field Guide to Island Nature

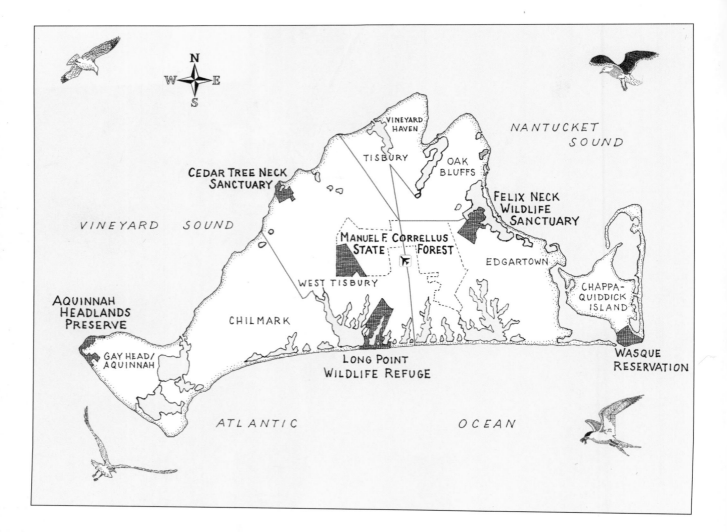

N W E S

VINEYARD HAVEN

TISBURY

OAK BLUFFS

CEDAR TREE NECK SANCTUARY

NANTUCKET SOUND

VINEYARD SOUND

FELIX NECK WILDLIFE SANCTUARY

MANUEL F. CORRELLUS STATE FOREST

WEST TISBURY

EDGARTOWN

AQUINNAH HEADLANDS PRESERVE

CHILMARK

CHAPPA-QUIDDICK ISLAND

GAY HEAD/ AQUINNAH

LONG POINT WILDLIFE REFUGE

WASQUE RESERVATION

ATLANTIC   OCEAN

MARTHA'S VINEYARD

A Field Guide to Island Nature

BY SUZAN BELLINCAMPI

DIRECTOR, MASS AUDUBON'S FELIX NECK WILDLIFE SANCTUARY

Mass Audubon
Protecting the Nature of Massachusetts

VINEYARD STORIES

Edgartown, Massachusetts

To those who have loved, protected, and inspired stewardship of Martha's Vineyard's land and waters and to everyone who will work for a vibrant Vineyard future.

And in memory of John Varkonda, Superintendent (1987–2013) of the Manuel Correllus State Forest who dedicated his life to those ideals.

Volume Copyright ©2014 Massachusetts Audubon Society

Published by Vineyard Stories
52 Bold Meadow Road
Edgartown, Massachusetts 02539
508-221-2338
www.vineyardstories.com

Library of Congress Number: 2014932077
ISBN: 978-0-9915028-0-6

An update of *Moraine to Marsh*, written by Anne Hale and published in 1988.

Reproduction of painting by Stan Murphy on page 92 is courtesy of the Murphy family.

Book Design: Jill Dible, Atlanta, Georgia

Printed in China

Contents

Introduction

||||||||||||||||||||||||||||||||||||||||||||||||||||||||||||||||||||||||||||||||||||||||||||||||||||||||||||||||||||||||||||||||||||||||||||||||||||||

**It is fortunate, perhaps, that no matter
how intently one studies the hundred
little dramas of the woods and meadows,
one can never learn all of the salient
facts about any one of them.**

—Aldo Leopold, conservationist, educator,
writer, and outdoor enthusiast

||||||||||||||||||||||||||||||||||||||||||||||||||||||||||||||||||||||||||||||||||||||||||||||||||||||||||||||||||||||||||||||||||||||||||||||||||||||

N 41°23', W 70°36' is currently the global address of Martha's Vineyard. With certainty, that address is changing, for this Island on the trailing edge of the North American continent moves westward an inch or so each year, or in the life span of an average person, the equivalent of one's height.

Lying just off the coast of southern Massachusetts, the Island nestles under the protecting arm of Cape Cod. In this nook, Martha's Vineyard avoids the cold Labrador Current sweeping down from the north and is bathed by trapped waters warmed by the Gulf Stream flowing from the south. This enviable geographic position gives the Vineyard its moderate climate. Winters tend to be milder than on the mainland; summers cooler. Spring comes more slowly, but autumn can be blissfully prolonged and warm compared with mainland regions of similar latitude.

Nearby are Nantucket and the Elizabeth Islands, which both share similarities to the Vineyard's geological history and climate. Nantucket lies to the east, further into the ocean and separated from the Vineyard by six-mile-wide Muskeget Channel; the chain of Elizabeth Islands runs southwest from Woods Hole, between the Vineyard and the mainland. Although all these islands possess many commonalities, there are significant differences.

The Vineyard is the largest of the islands; it also has the greatest topographic relief, boasts more and taller trees, and has a larger variety of flora and fauna. The famous colored cliffs at Gay Head / Aquinnah are perhaps the most striking and well-known natural feature of the Vineyard and may be the largest display of ancient sediments from the Pleistocene era (approximately 2,588,000 to 11,700 years ago) to be found anywhere in the world.

Sandy beaches and many sheltered harbors, combined with the pleasant climate and warm waters, make this one of the finest resort areas on the northeastern coast. The delights of the Vineyard draw an ever-increasing number of visitors and residents. Yet many who come may miss one of the rarest treats the Island can afford: the pleasure of getting to know more about nature.

Martha's Vineyard: A Field Guide to Island Nature explains the geological past of Cape Cod and the islands from the time mountains rose from the sea to the period when the land masses became separate entities. This background will help you to see the Island

hills and plains from the more than 200-million-year perspective of its known geological history and to appreciate the forces that created its foundations.

Changes that have taken place since the last glacier began retreating about 16,000 years ago produced the habitats of the Island's current ecosystem—habitats that include the abundantly rich salt marshes, the mature woodlands of the moraines, the special sand plains, and the dynamic ocean beaches where major alterations can occur in a matter of hours rather than centuries.

And as the climate continues to change, shifts in ranges of plants and wildlife are occurring. Observable differences in phenology (the science of the interaction of climate and biological occurrences such as migrations and plant leaf out and flowering) are being noted and studied.

This book can be your guide as you explore the Island. It will take you literally and figuratively from moraine to marsh—from a description of the formation of the oldest part of the Island, its moraines, to the development of the salt marsh, the Island's youngest land formation.

Blue flag iris

Information provided here will teach you to recognize some of the plants and animals as you walk the trails. The six trail guides, along with the maps and specific information on what you will see, will lead you to beautiful vistas—visual and perhaps spiritual. The Tips for Trips scattered around the book will help keep you safe.

The final chapters of the book, "Beetlebung" and "Pinkletink," are guides to Island flora and fauna and identifies the most common and conspicuous plants and animals found here—most of those that you are likely to see. A few unusual or endangered species are included, too. Keys facilitate the identification of shells, trees, and shrubs.

An old saying goes, "You can never step in a river in the same place twice." Similarly, you can never walk the same trail twice. Natural processes are working constantly, even as they did in the past, to bring about further change on the Vineyard—sometimes slowly and sometimes quickly, but relentlessly to be sure.

Enjoy your adventures around the Island. It is quite a place.

CHAPTER ONE

The Hidden History of Martha's Vineyard

Every single thing changes and is changing always in this world.
Yet with the same light the moon goes on shining.

—Saigyo, Japanese Poet

> **When the glaciers melted, rising waters flooded the land until only the highest peaks remained above sea level. These elevated lands now surrounded by water became the island we now know as Martha's Vineyard.**

In geological terms, Martha's Vineyard is a youngster. Its foundations are 200 million years old, but its existence as an island is less than 10,000 years. Its story is one of land and water in a battle for dominance, of great glaciations and tumultuous melting, and of time and change.

The ocean may someday again swallow the Island. It is possible that in another 10,000 years, this land could lie beneath the sea again. Perhaps in an interim period it will exist as Skiff's Island off Wasque on Chappaquiddick does today—sometimes an island, sometimes a shoal.

Cyclical periods throughout the earth's history show that continents stood high as mountains rose, glaciers and deserts formed, and seas remained well-confined within their basins. In succeeding periods, erosion ate away at the mountains, glaciers melted, and the rising sea inundated all but the most elevated lands.

Martha's Vineyard was not excluded from these processes. Change is constant here.

The earth's seemingly solid crust is made up of drifting tectonic plates. Ancient mountains, now eroded beneath Martha's Vineyard, resulted from complex geological activities triggered when the plates carrying the continents of the world last drifted together in the early Paleozoic Era (approximately 570 million to 240 million years ago) and formed a single supercontinent, Pangaea. In the later Jurassic period (205 million to 138 million years ago), the plates separated again and the continents began to move to their present locations. The North American continental plate continues to slowly drift westward each year.

Bedrock, a component of the tectonic plates, is hard to come by on the Vineyard. Although bedrock on the mainland is easily seen, the Island's bedrock is buried under several hundred feet of sediments. These sediments were eventually pushed and pried by the giant glaciers that once covered these lands.

Over the millennia the constantly restless relationship between sea and land produced layers of new deposits on the bedrock of the continental shelf. Each layer represents a period when specific environmental conditions prevailed and left their signature in the deposits and fossils unique to that time. While such sediments underlie the whole area, only some from the Cretaceous and the late Tertiary period are visible today—in the colorful cliffs of Gay Head / Aquinnah.

The earliest deposits are clays and lignites—soft, brownish-black coal deposits. These can be found at the lowest levels of the cliffs and contain vegetative remains from the Cretaceous period (138 million to 66 million years ago), which included the presence of giant animals like dinosaurs. They reveal the existence of an ancient forest and the arrival of modern hardwood trees that were later drowned when the sea rose again.

The end of the Cretaceous period, when the sea level fell and volcanoes were active, was an occasion for dramatic change for all life on earth, as many plants and animals, including the dinosaurs, became extinct. Older kinds of plants disappeared, and flowering plants bearing nuts, fruit, and grains came into their own. The plants were accompanied by newly evolved animals, mammals that roamed the recently bared coastal plain.

Mammals rapidly increased in numbers and species as they adapted to feeding on the new growth.

The Cretaceous period ended with another worldwide phase of mountain building and the withdrawal of the widespread sea. During this time, revolutionary

Megalodon tooth

changes were taking place in the physical environment of the earth and its life-forms, ushering in the Cenozoic Era of modern life 66 million years ago.

As the sea withdrew, the land along the New England coast was exposed once more, and forest trees again flourished. By the Miocene epoch (23 million to 5.3 million years ago), another inundation spread a shallow sea over the coastal plain on which the Vineyard would later rise. In its marine deposits, the shallow greensands, many fossils suggest that the climate here was warm and pleasant. But that was about to change.

By the beginning of the Pleistocene epoch, considered the last ice age, a major transformation began. The climate cooled so radically that season after season passed when more snow fell than melted. Snow accumulated over the Laurentian Mountains in northern Canada, forming a great continental ice sheet. This, in time, spawned glaciers that spread southward in fits and starts, finally reaching as far as northern New Jersey.

During the million or more years the Island lay under glacial siege, the climate was cold. Bitter winds howled, creating an inhospitable environment for any form of life. All the plants, oaks included, were driven southward along with the dependent animals.

What a sight it must have been!

The glaciers intermittently covered this region. Between glacial advances were periods when the ice would retreat for tens of thousands of years, freeing the land of its cover until another surge carried the ice back again. The glaciers passed over the coastal plain a number of times before taking what was probably their final leave about 20,000 years ago. The exact stopping place for each forward movement of the glaciers is unknown.

Picture a wall of ice thousands of feet high with roaring torrents of water pouring off the top and out of streams within the ice, torrents that increased in volume and speed as the climate moderated. Imagine bitter, fierce winds shrieking off the glacier, blowing sand across the outwash plains where stones, rocks, and boulders were sandblasted into forms still evident today.

Sometimes the glaciers reached far across the coastal plain past where the Vineyard is today, erasing evidence of earlier glaciations.

As the glaciers advanced, they lifted from the mainland everything they could pry loose. Soil, rock, and vegetation were pushed to the very outer edges of the ice and deposited on the preglacial sediments of the continental shelf. The glacial deposits ultimately formed the Cape and islands, creating the moraine, or structural backbone of the region.

Had this pirated cargo not been dumped here, the entire area would still lie beneath the returning postglacial sea.

The new glacial deposits—a moraine of a long windrow of rock, and the delta-like outwash plain—lay bare. The glacier retreated northward and wasted away, and the warming climate along with the new access to light and air permitted life to resume in the wake of the waning ice. Plant communities returned to the Island in successive stages and clothed the bare landforms over the ensuing thousands of years.

PLANTS AND ANIMALS REPOPULATE THE ISLAND The first plants that could endure the still severe climate in the aftermath of the glaciers were similar to those now found in the arctic tundra and on alpine mountaintops: lichens, grasses, sedges, dwarf trees, and shrubs—plant species that can grow where the ground is frozen most of the year and the amount of sunlight is limited. As the climate warmed, forests of spruce and fir replaced the tundra growth and blanketed the Vineyard landforms.

By the time the ice had retreated to its present Arctic position, summers were hot although winters remained cold. Conditions then favored broadleaf trees that could utilize the increasing supply of water and nutrients released during the longer periods of frost-free weather. Forests became established in New England, and the

oaks, so prominent on the Vineyard today, made their first appearance on the Island. These trees were able to shed their leaves in cold weather as a protection from desiccation when water was frozen in the ground.

Martha's Vineyard today appears covered mostly with oak trees. These trees dominate the Vineyard's woodlands as nature reclaims lands less managed by

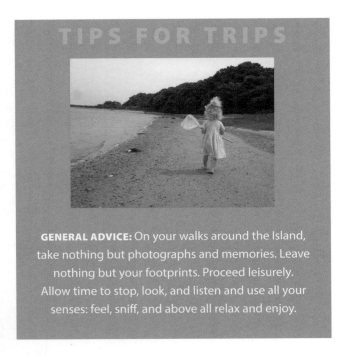

TIPS FOR TRIPS

GENERAL ADVICE: On your walks around the Island, take nothing but photographs and memories. Leave nothing but your footprints. Proceed leisurely. Allow time to stop, look, and listen and use all your senses: feel, sniff, and above all relax and enjoy.

GLACIERS: THE ICY STORY OF OUR PAST

The Vineyard's topography—with its hills, ponds, cliffs, and coastal sculpture—is a direct result of the glacier that moved through New England.

When the ancient ice sheet grew, it locked more and more of earth's water in its grip, and the sea level fell. The coastline lay near the edge of the continental shelf, far beyond its present location. Glacial deposits had formed a series of foothills on the wide coastal plain bordering the mainland. When the ice began to melt, it released large quantities of water, raising the level of the sea.

Gradually the meeting place of sea and land moved inland, with waters flooding over the continental shelf onto the New England coastal plain. When the sea reached the morainal deposits, it stopped until it found low places where it could pass between the highlands. The isolated areas of coastal plain that it surrounded became the Islands and Cape Cod. The lowlands between the ranges of hilly moraines and the mainland became Nantucket Sound, Vineyard Sound, and Buzzards Bay.

At the sea's return, the shoreline of the Island looked entirely different from today. Instead of the gentle arc of South Beach, the sea met a ragged edge of land. Points of higher terrain jutted into the ocean, connected in time by the action of currents.

At first, spits formed to the east of the points of land; as more and more sand was carried along by the currents, the spits extended until the projecting hills were linked by a barrier beach. The bays closed off from the ocean became the ponds that currently lie behind the majestic curve of South Beach. Lore has it that 200 years ago, it was possible to ice skate from Tisbury Great Pond to Edgartown on the frozen ponds behind and north of the barrier beach.

The barrier beaches of Sengekontacket and Tashmoo Ponds were formed by similar currents, as was the spit of land that closes off Lagoon Pond on the eastern shore of Vineyard Haven harbor and supports the roadway connecting Oak Bluffs and Vineyard Haven.

THE ISLAND LOSES REAL ESTATE These currents are still reshaping the islands and Cape Cod, slowly and irrevocably whittling away at their edges. With each tide the ocean nips away a little beach. Frequently losses are major, and large sections of land disappear quickly, especially during storms. Losses in one place can sometimes lead to gains elsewhere. But overall the Island is gradually losing its real estate in the never-ending tug of war between land and sea.

The progress of erosion can be slow or fast, as in the case of storms. Its effects are easily seen on the Island, especially on the south shore. Many houses have been moved farther back from the land's edge, though perhaps the most massive and memorable relocation was that of a house and guest house on Wasque on Chappaquiddick. At this writing, the Gay Head Lighthouse is under threat, and plans are under way to move the historic structure. Another notable and, for many, devastating loss occurred at Lucy Vincent Beach, where the cliffs have seemingly melted away.

Today, climate change is having an effect on Vineyard habitats and wildlife. *Climate change* describes long-term alterations in climate due to the warming of the earth resulting from human activities that increase the release of greenhouse gasses. Some observable and predictable events include the northward range shifts of birds, fish, and other organisms; earlier flowering of plants; and earlier breeding of wildlife. The shrinking of glaciers that had retreated to the world's poles now causes a rise in sea level that will drastically change Island and mainland shorelines where the majority of people live.

These processes will continue. In a few thousand more years, the Island may become a baring shoal and, eventually, just another sandbar along the coast of southern New England.

Red cedar and butterfly weed

humans. Cedars and pines still grow in open land where there is full sun and the oaks have yet to invade. Sassafras appears in the lowlands, and beetlebungs and red maples in wetlands. Where oaks are absent, it is only a matter of time before they appear. Only salt marshes, eroding beaches, and eroding cliffs are excepted from the process.

Oaks, however, have not always been the dominant trees here. One hundred million years ago, long before the glaciers' arrival, ancestors of the oaks had only just evolved. Over 100 species of trees have been identified from the plant remains preserved when the sea flooded inland and submerged the ancient forests.

A UNIQUE ISLAND The animals that historically inhabited this area also began to expand their southern ranges and to recolonize northern regions. This time, humans, a new class of mammals, came with them, tracking the mammoth and mastodon. Our fauna expanded and presently include some species less common to our mainland neighbors. Among those are birds such as barn owls, short-eared owls, and northern harriers. The imperial moth and the northeastern tiger beetle are rare insects adapted to special Island habitats or simply those whose populations have outlived their mainland relatives.

Many flora absent or infrequently found on the mainland can be seen here on the Island, this patch of unique coastal plain. Among them are Nantucket shadbush, butterfly weed, wood lily, bushy rock rose, a sandplain blue-eyed grass, and broom crowberry.

The presence of these and other plant and animal species suggest that the current assemblage of Vineyard flora and fauna is truly unique.

Microclimatic differences in soil types, the availability of moisture, and changes in exposure and temperature provide conditions that allow different kinds of plants to grow. Areas where climate favors the dominance of certain plants and limits the growth of other types are called biomes. Within each biome, species other than the dominant ones are also to be found.

Within New England, two distinct types of major plant associations are found. The northern tier of states is distinguished by sugar maple and white birch. In the southern three states, mixed oak forests dominate. Nowhere is the line between these two plant associations straight or clear, and associations mingle in some places.

Imperial moth caterpillars

Here on the coastal plain, although climatic conditions are similar to the rest of southern New England, the soils are porous and drain quickly. Trees are unable to reach the height or develop the multilayered understory beneath their canopy that represents a true New England forest. The mature vegetation on the Island is better described as woodlands.

While the moraine and outwash were being cloaked by successive plant associations, two significant marine landforms were evolving—one less dramatic than the other, but no less interesting. The ocean rising with the meltwater from the glaciers reached new levels, flooded farther and farther inland, and created constantly changing interfaces between the sea and land.

The most exciting interface exists where the ocean is in direct contact with the land. Here the balance between forces shifts frequently and life is precarious. Only life-forms equipped to resist abrasion, desiccation, and salt poisoning can endure. Those less hardy species must be capable of retreating when conditions

Sengekontacket pond

become unfavorable. Nowhere are the dynamics of erosion and deposition better displayed than in ocean interface regions where air and water currents regularly construct and destroy shore features.

In the quieter waters of salt ponds and lagoons, where barrier beaches offer protection from ocean waves, salt marshes formed. The richness of this youngest of the Island's terrains is unequaled in our hemisphere.

Archaeological research suggests that the first Native American encampments on the Island's coasts may now lie beneath the ocean.

CHAPTER TWO

A Key to Vineyard Landscapes

I only went out for a walk and finally concluded to stay out till sundown, for going out, I found, was really going in.

----John Muir

At first glance, the Island's landscapes, while still somewhat rural in character, might appear all the same. Yet the seeming uniformity of pitch pine and oak masks a wide variety of different habitats contained within its special insular ecosystem.

A rocky beach abuts a sandy shore. A grassy hill suddenly has an outcropping of huge rocks called erratics. A calm freshwater pond is just over a dune from a surging oceanfront.

This guide helps you read the Island's landscapes and see deeper into its very special ecological places.

WOODLANDS The Vineyard provides a historical example of succession from open land to woodlands. Early settlers clear-cut most of the virgin forest they found on the Island. They sought open space for pastures and crops, and they needed wood to build homes and boats, as well as fuel for heat and power. The size and kinds of woodland trees visible today roughly indicates the amount of time that has passed since the land was used for agriculture.

Succession on the Vineyard from bare ground or neglected agricultural land begins with pioneer plants, which are able to first colonize disrupted or damaged landscapes. In the Island's dry and porous soils, the pioneer plants often include lichens (reindeer moss in particular), annual herbaceous plants, and tenacious grasses such as poverty grass or little bluestem.

Fields no longer kept open or farmed return in stages to oak-dominated woodlands. Typically red cedars first punctuate unattended fields. Often woody shrubs, beach plums, bayberry, and huckleberry are found in thickets and the edges of the woodland and field interface.

Steeplebush

Pitch pines appear next. When the rapidly growing pines become numerous and tall enough, they shade out the red cedars. The demise of the pines occurs as the oaks repeat the process, first mixing with, then overshadowing the pines. In the older climax woodlands, beeches and hickories are found with the oaks. They are frequently seen Up-Island, especially in areas protected by glacial push-ridges from strong prevailing winds and in more moisture-retentive soils.

FRESHWATER PONDS Where land interfaces with bodies of fresh water, as in ponds and streams, decaying vegetation slowly raises the level of the pond bottom and accumulates at its edges. The water body gradually becomes smaller and shallower with age and sediment deposition. Eventually bog or swamp conditions are reached, with each stage distinguished by its own community of plants and animals.

As the process continues, wetland herbs and shrubs enter and add their decaying remains to the soil. In time they will be replaced by wetland trees. Finally, shrubs adapted to drier soils and pines and oaks may grow where once there was a pond.

Look at any pond for emergent plants and other signs of succession. The ponds at Cedar Tree Neck (Ames Pond) and Felix Neck (Turtle Pond and Bog

Pitch pines

Pond) show their place in the process. The last is in an advanced stage of succession to bog.

SALT WATER TO MARSHES At places that bodies of salt water are protected from pounding surf, salt marshes flourish and in turn buffer the land behind them. As the grasses and other plants of the salt marsh die back each year, their decaying remains add to the accumulating peat of the marsh. In infinitesimal layers, the edges of saltwater bodies build outward and the surface level of the peat rises.

The cordgrass at the water's edge moves to fill new niches in the marsh; salt meadow grass, which is adapted to living where high tides often flow, moves in behind the cordgrass as marsh levels rise. Plants such as spike grass and black grass, normally found farther back on the marsh and reached only by storm tides, creep forward; marsh elder and groundsel bush on the inland edge of the marsh move to take their place.

At each stage, decaying plant species prepare the way for others to follow. The process thus continues until the environment eventually supports shrubs and trees, and woodlands become established. The marsh enlarges and prospers as it gradually encroaches on areas of open water, and the nearby woodlands slowly expand.

OCEANS AND BEACHES On South Beach, people may swim next year where you stroll today. As the ocean beach erodes under forces created by wind-driven waves and the action of currents, the dunes behind the beach move inland, encroaching on the heathlands.

Long Point is a good example. As you walk back through the landward-shifting dune area you will spot land-building plant associations that are moving toward the beach. In the open heathlands, clumps of scrubby thickets appear that will increase in size until they support oak woodlands. The wooded section of the trail to the

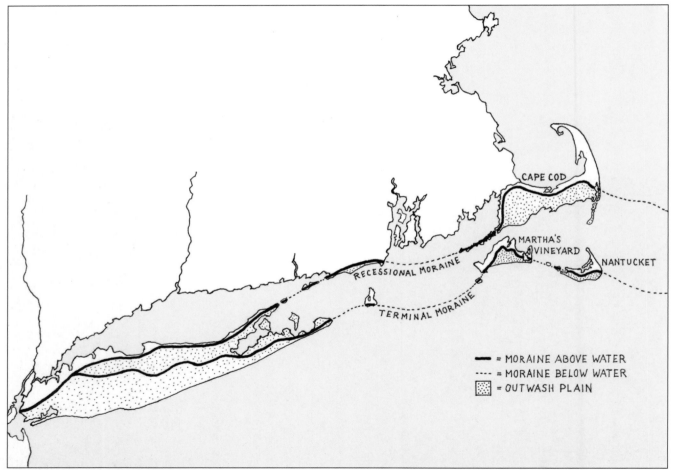

Outer limits of moraines and outwash plain

winterside parking lot will have lengthened perceptibly in a few decades as the woodland creeps toward the beach.

Cliffs also play a major role in the loss of land to the sea. Although it may seem that the sea eats away at the toe of the cliff, causing its collapse, more often the primary agent of loss is water seeping from the water table in the upper levels of the cliffs. Slick areas are created, and large sections of cliff crash to the beach below. Then the sea takes over, removing the debris and carrying it away. This process can be observed at the Gay Head Cliffs.

MORAINES The most significant gift of the glaciers is the terminal moraine, the backbone of the Island. Moraines comprise heavier deposits—rocks and coarser stones—carried by the glacial ice and only the fastest flowing water. Think of a bulldozer pushing dirt and rocks, with the moraine represented by the pile of dirt and rocks in front of the machine, and the bulldozer as the glacier.

Terminal moraines mark the farthest advance of the glaciers. The highest terrain of the Vineyard is a terminal moraine. The Elizabeth Islands constitute a recessional moraine and define the place where the retreating glacier stopped briefly.

A characteristic of land in the moraine is the presence of clay and large rocks and boulders. Clay retains water in the soil and traps it. Water contained near the surface forms bogs, swamps, ponds, and streams. A greater variety of trees and taller growth is supported by the more moisture-holding soil. The rocks and boulders left by the flowing waters of the melting glaciers provided

TIPS FOR TRIPS

TICKS: Three kinds of ticks have been reported on the Island: dog tick, deer tick, and most recently, lone star tick. They can transmit five different kinds of diseases: Lyme disease, babesiosis, anaplasmosis, tularemia, Rocky Mountain spotted fever, and ehrlichiosis.

Insect repellent protects against mosquitoes and discourages ticks if applied liberally around the ankles and lower legs. You gain further protection if you wear long pants and tuck them into your socks.

Check yourself carefully upon returning home if you have walked through woods, fields, or beach grass areas. Don't panic if you find a tick. It usually takes several hours (most experts say 24 hours) before a tick's bite does any harm.

For further and more detailed (and local) information on ticks and the illnesses that they can transmit, go to http://www.mvboh.org/tbioverview.

materials for the stone walls that are frequently seen on morainal Up-Island land and seldom Down-Island.

OUTWASH The Vineyard outwash plain lies south of the moraine and covers much of its eastern end. It is clay-poor, instead made up of a huge spread of finer sands and gravels, pulverized from the tumbling rocks and stones. These lighter materials flowed with the meltwater streams far beyond the ice front and were deposited in a deltalike formation that extended well out to sea from the present coastline.

The paths of the old glacial meltwater streambeds, now called *bottoms* or *frost bottoms*, can still be traced in topographic maps as they cross the outwash plain. They run southward until they reach sea level, where they form the basins of the ponds behind the south shore of the Island. The West Tisbury–Edgartown Road provides a profile of these contours. When driving a car or riding a bicycle along that road or the adjoining bike path, you can experience for yourself the configurations of the outwash plain—the dips into the bottoms and rises on the highlands between them. Deep Bottom, about a mile west of the entrance to the airport, is indeed the deepest and also the steepest.

The sand and gravels of the outwash plain facilitate the rapid percolation of water that quickly becomes unavailable to plants. This condition is revealed in the sand plains, which are dominated by scrub and post oak and pitch pine and known by anyone who has tried to plant a garden in these soils.

Beneath the outwash plain is the Island's largest supply of fresh water—its aquifer. Soil saturated with water

GLACIAL JIGSAW PUZZLE

Glaciers move with a scalloped edge, in lobes rather than as a single wall of ice. Two lobes of the Wisconsin Glacier put the finishing touches on Martha's Vineyard. The slightly earlier Cape Cod lobe formed the eastern section of the Vineyard moraine. It stretches from Chappaquiddick along the north shore of Edgartown to the eastern shore of Lagoon Pond between Vineyard Haven and Oak Bluffs. The later Buzzards Bay lobe is responsible for the western section of the moraine, the high lands that run from West Chop along the north shore to Aquinnah. The earlier Illinoian glacier had already left the moraine that underlies Noman's Land, Squibnocket, and some Up-Island hills.

underlies the whole Island. Some of it is salt water; some fresh renewed only by rainfall. Since fresh water is lighter than salt water, it floats on top. The State Forest covers much of the aquifer and acts as a natural recharge area.

The freshwater supply Up-Island is under the moraine away from the outwash plain. There, water is contained in relatively small pockets of clay, some near the surface, some very deep.

OTHER GLACIAL SOUVENIRS

Gay Head/Aquinnah Cliffs The most exciting and stunning reminder of our glacial history is the cliff area at Gay Head / Aquinnah, where pressure from the moving Illinoian and Wisconsin glaciers forced a million centuries of preglacial deposits upward, exposing them as they folded and faulted, much like ribbon candy. These deformed sediments reveal the geological past of the Island in a layered mixture of sand, gravel, and clay. Some contain fossils, others boulders; together they display a virtual rainbow of colors.

The mid-Cretaceous clays and lignites at the base of the Gay Head Cliffs indicate that familiar-looking trees grew in ancient forests—ancestors of pines, hollies, and sassafras.

Higher in the cliffs at Gay Head / Aquinnah are the greensands left 40 million years later, during the

Gay Head/Aquinnah cliffs

Miocene epoch. The greensands—the name reflects their color—reveal that the climate was warm and the sea flooded the coastal plain. Fossilized teeth and bones suggest that giant sharks hunted a variety of sea mammals and fish.

Geologists have reconstructed the chronology of the cliffs despite gaps in the record. Although interpretations vary, geologists now read the many-hued layers like pages in a history book. Hidden history has resurfaced.

Kettle Holes At times, huge blocks of ice broke away from the face of the melting glacier and became buried in its outwash. Thus insulated, they melted more slowly than the rest of the ice and eventually left depressions called kettle holes in the surface of the land. Where the kettle holes are deep and lie below the level of the water table, they are seen as small inland ponds. Dodger's Hole (alongside the Vineyard Haven–Edgartown Road near the Oak Bluffs–Edgartown line) and Little Pond in the State Forest are examples.

Erratics The occasional large isolated rock that you might see on the Vineyard is a piece of mainland bedrock that was transported by the glaciers more than 20,000 years ago.

Erratic

These rocks, called glacial erratics, were bulldozed and conveyed by the moving ice and often are of impressive size. They are found on the Island's surface mostly in the western end of the moraine. In the eastern section of the Island, a few erratics have been unearthed from beneath the outwash plain during building projects. Look for a small erratic at the entrance to Felix Neck, which was uncovered when electric lines were laid, or go to the Martha's Vineyard Land Bank's Waskosim's Rock Reservation to find other examples.

Ventifacts The small erratic at the entrance to Felix Neck has a double life: it is also a ventifact, a special rock shaped by wind-driven sand. Before the outwash from the Buzzards Bay lobe of the glacier covered it, the rock lay on the sandy surface just in front of the Cape Cod glacial lobe. Then the rock spent centuries being reshaped.

You can identify ventifacts most easily by touch. Characteristically they have a smooth, satiny finish on flat, faceted planes, with a raised "keel" or ridge between them. Smaller specimens can be seen in most outwash plain areas wherever glacial drift—a mixture of pebbles and rocks—occurs. Ventifacts are often found along the shores of shallow bays and lagoons, inland on fire trails in the State Forest, and on the Felix Neck trail described in this guide.

CHAPTER THREE

Walking the Island's Trails

Adopt the pace of nature; her secret is patience.

—Ralph Waldo Emerson

||||||||||||||||||||||||||||||||||||||||||||||||||||||||||||||||||||||||||||||||||||||||||||||||||||||||||||||||||||||||||||||||||||||||||||||||||||

A favorite among Islanders for its magical woodlands and spectacular views.

||||||||||||||||||||||||||||||||||||||||||||||||||||||||||||||||||||||||||||||||||||||||||||||||||||||||||||||||||||||||||||||||||||||||||||||||||||

Cedar Tree Neck Sanctuary

―――――――――――――――――――――― FAST FACTS ――――――――――――――――――――――

MAILING ADDRESS: Sheriff's Meadow Foundation Wakeman Center / 57 David Avenue / Vineyard Haven, MA 02568

SITE ADDRESS: The terminus of Obed Daggett Road / West Tisbury, MA

CONTACT: 508.693.5207 / info@sheriffsmeadow.org • **OWNERSHIP:** Sheriff's Meadow Foundation

NUMBER OF ACRES: 312 • www.sheriffsmeadow.org

Cedar Tree Neck showcases meandering streams, groves of pygmy beech trees, freshwater ponds and bogs, and a spectacular panoramic view of the Elizabeth Islands.

Amenities: The sanctuary is open from 8:30 am to 5:30 pm, every day. Swimming is not permitted at Cedar Tree Neck. Dogs on leash only permitted; dogs prohibited on the beach when shorebirds are nesting (April 1 through September 1).

Directions: From its intersection with State Road, follow Indian Hill Road for 1.3 miles. Turn right onto the Obed Daggett Road (near the hilltop). Follow the "Sanctuary" signs, taking Obed Daggett Road 1 mile to its terminus at the Cedar Tree Neck trailhead and parking area. This hilly entrance road can be very challenging on foot and by bicycle.

HISTORY The Wampanoag called Cedar Tree Neck "Squemmechchue" (red fruit land), referring to the cranberries that grew wild there.

The Mayhew Norton family farmed these lands after the Wampanoag and sold land to the Daggett family in the late 1800s. The Daggetts lived at Cedar Tree Neck for generations. For many years they maintained a small inn, serving meals in the main house to their guests, who rented small cottages close by. This group of buildings can be seen from the bluff that overlooks

Vineyard Sound. The story of the simple life of this old Island clan is told in the book *It Began with a Whale*, published by John Daggett in 1963.

Cedar Tree Neck Sanctuary, which includes the Obed Sherman and Maria Roberts Daggett Sanctuary, was acquired through a cooperative fund-raising campaign by the Sheriff's Meadow Foundation and Mass Audubon. The below-market price of $165,000 seemed an immense amount for 100 acres in the mid-1960s.

Contiguous to the original part of the sanctuary is the Alexander Reed Bird Refuge, acquired through gifts from the Norton and Alexander S. Reed families. A final parcel that abuts Seven Gates is called Fish Hook and was gifted by Henry and George Hough.

The late Henry Beetle Hough, writer and longtime editor of the *Vineyard Gazette*, often walked the trails of Cedar Tree Neck Sanctuary with his dogs. The Hough homestead abutted the sanctuary. Henry grew up here on the Island; he knew these hills and dells intimately and loved them dearly.

Throughout his life, Hough distinguished himself by his writing and his other stalwart efforts to protect the beauty and character of Martha's Vineyard. A Pulitzer Prize winner and a former president of the Henry Thoreau Society, Henry Hough was the recipient of

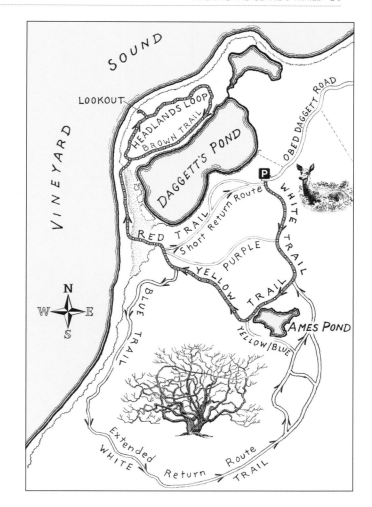

> ❝ My first impulse, as I drew in the delight of that scene, was to thank the Lord for Henry Hough, for his comprehension, his patient impatience . . . and his love for the Island. I recalled what he had said once about how he knew he couldn't solve all of the problems of this world, but he would settle for improving and protecting a small part of it. . . . If for no other reason than the joy of this morning's ramble, I am grateful to you. ❞
>
> —David E. Lilienthal, a Cedar Tree Neck neighbor of Henry Beetle Hough, founder of Sheriff's Meadow

many prestigious awards for his environmental work as well as his literary productions.

Island historian and passionate defender, he chronicled the essence of the Vineyard as he lived it through his many books. Henry Beetle Hough's energy, foresight, and dedication to conservation in large part made this sanctuary a reality. It abuts the Seven Gates Farm property and other large land holdings to the west, which are under conservation restrictions, thus protecting a large segment of the north shore of the Island.

NATURAL FEATURES In this sanctuary a wide diversity of habitats are present: mature woodlands, freshwater ponds and wetlands, a beach, dunes, and a bluff on a headland that projects farther into Vineyard Sound than any other place along the north shore between Gay Head and West Chop. A magnificent panorama of the Elizabeth Islands is visible from the bluff.

The natural features of Cedar Tree Neck are typical of Up-Island and the western moraine and differ from those Down-Island, as seen at Felix Neck. The topography here is steeper. Extensive networks of fresh water and occasional large erratics, boulders left here by the glaciers, are found.

When you walk the trails, the many ridges and valleys in this sanctuary become apparent. Some are preglacial deposits that were folded as the glacier, which acted like a bulldozer, pushed against them. Others were deposits laid down as the ice paused during its uneven retreat.

Many types of freshwater habitats lie within the folds of land: streams, brooks, freshwater ponds, swamps, and bogs—as great a variety of wetlands as can be found in any one area open to the public on Martha's Vineyard. Plants and associated fauna specific to these habitats are abundant.

The sanctuary's woodlands are among the most mature woodlands on the Island. Most of the trees are oaks, but characteristic of the western moraine, other tree species live in these older woods. Some of the Vineyard's finest stands of beech flourish here. Sassafras and hickory grow in the lowland woodlands, while red maple and beetlebung populate the wetter habitats.

Stone walls course through the property. Though they seem to run aimlessly uphill and down through the woodlands, they mark the boundaries of former pasturelands and remain as testaments to the strong backs and hard work of the early settlers. Many deer live along the north shore where there are open woodlands, development is tightly controlled, and hunting is limited.

You are unlikely to see an abundance of birds in the deep woods during the day. In the daylight hours they frequent edges in search of food, so look for them in

hedges, thickets, and along the shoreline. Look and listen for the black-capped chickadee and the white-breasted nuthatch, both year-rounders. Woodpeckers, perhaps the hairy—more likely the smaller downy—will also be about. Keep an eye out for the northern flicker and for the scarlet tanager, an uncommon summer visitor that prefers deciduous woodlands and has been seen and heard along the trails on the upper part of the sanctuary.

The sanctuary has been set aside for wildlife study and preservation, not as a recreational facility. Allow adequate time to explore. Although the shorter walk option takes a bit more than an hour including brief stops at points of interest, this unique refuge invites dalliance to savor the peace and relative solitude.

TRAIL GUIDE

Before you start, look in the kiosk for maps, guides, and other relevant information. Grab a sanctuary map to orient yourself to the starting point and its relationship to the rest of the sanctuary. There are several trails to follow, incentives for repeated visits.

Two trails lead out of the parking area. The Red Trail, on your right when facing the kiosk, goes directly to the beach and bluff. **Take the White Trail**, which begins at the southeastern or left side of the kiosk.

As you walk up the White Trail, look for sassafras trees. You can easily recognize them by their three different shapes of leaves. Sassafras, *Sassafras albidum*, is identified by these distinct leaf shapes: a simple football-shaped leaf, a mittenlike leaf with two lobes, and another with three lobes resembling a ghost. In the tradition of the gold rush that helped to open the West, this tree was the "gold" that first attracted Europeans to Martha's Vineyard. Because of its reputed medicinal properties, sassafras was much valued in the early 17th century. How things can change! Today sassafras is considered by some to be carcinogenic. Crush a leaf or break a twig off to smell its refreshing lemony fragrance. Some people disregard the warnings and use its roots to make sassafras candy, or its leaves for tea or as a thickener known in the South as filé powder.

The introduced red pines have not fared well, as the many dead and dying trees show. These trees are not native to the Vineyard and were planted here. They do better in more northern climes, preferring colder conditions.

Pass the Purple Trail that forks to the right and **continue a short distance to the intersection with the Yellow Trail. Take this second right-hand fork, the Yellow (Irons) Trail,** and go down a slight incline. (It takes four to five minutes from the parking area to reach this point.) The Yellow Trail is also part of the Bruce Irons Trail, and an educational brochure available at the kiosk, designed especially for children, details features along the route. Bruce Irons was

Sassafras leaves

an educator who loved the Vineyard and cared deeply about protecting and conserving it.

The trail shortly enters a grove of tall beech trees on the left; beeches typically grow in such groups. If you are lucky, you can find beechdrops, a small plant that grows from the beech's root on the earth's surface. This plant, *Epifagus virginiana*, is a beech-root parasite. Beechdrops can only survive in conjunction with beech trees since they cannot photosynthesize and must get their nutrients from their host tree.

Beech, *Fagus grandifolia*, is easily identified by the smooth gray bark; the alternately arranged, coarsely toothed, light green leaves; and the handsome slender buds. Resist the urge to carve in the bark as others have done; consider the injury to the tree and the scar on this pristine landscape. Beeches are often found in the western moraine, though some beech trees are in the woods east of the roundabout on the Vineyard Haven–Edgartown Road.

Beeches are among the few trees that reproduce well in shade. Young trees grow from root sprouts along the shallow root system of the mother plant as well as from seed (attractive four-sectioned, woody husks). Because the root sprouts receive nourishment from the mature tree, they can grow more quickly under new openings in the canopy and soon overshadow competitors.

Beech tree

Just beyond the beech grove is Ames Pond, named for a neighbor of the sanctuary who was a friend of Henry Beetle Hough. Approach quietly and look carefully. Except in winter when they are down at the bottom of the pond, a painted turtle or two can sometimes be seen lounging in the sun. The turtle will probably splash into the water once it becomes aware of your presence. Stop here for a few minutes to enjoy this tranquil spot.

Ames Pond is a favorite area for visitors in any season. Memorable experiences are available here throughout the year. Listen to the pinkletink frog chorus in March and April, watch the tadpoles on the bottom of the pond in spring, or admire the activities of the water

Ames pond

insects in summer. You can catch the delicious scent of the swamp azalea and sweet pepperbush in summer, or feast your eyes in early autumn on the first fall colors of the beetlebungs and red maples. In winter, enjoy the quiet isolation and search for animal tracks along the pond's edge when there is snow.

Look for two native trees—beetlebung, of which there are three located to the right of the dam, and a red maple located at the water's edge. Beetlebung, *Nyssa sylvatica*, is the Island name for the tupelo or black gum tree of the mainland. A tree of the wetland community, it usually grows in groves or thickets, as at Beetlebung Corner in Chilmark.

Notice the characteristic habit of growing long, slender, nearly horizontal branches, with short, spur-like twigs. The leaves are simple, alternate, and are a rich green in color. Where exposed to wind and spray, the particular habit of growth and rounded outline of beetlebung groves is distinctive and serves for identification when the leaves have fallen.

The tree's name derives from the usage of the wood. The colonists made bungs for corking barrels from it, as well as beetles, or mallets, to drive them into place. The wood is tough and dense, and since it tends to absorb less water than other woods, beetlebung corks were preferred for ease in the uncorking operation.

Red or swamp maple, *Acer rubrum*, is easy to identify by looking at its leaves, which are the characteristic three-pointed "maple" shape. Notice that the leaves grow opposite each other, and that the twigs and branches do likewise. Only a few trees have this pattern of growth. More commonly, leaves, twigs, and branches are arranged in an alternate pattern.

Red maple is an appropriate name since that color appears on some part of the tree in almost every season. The red is most conspicuous in the fall. It is one of the first trees to show color and is among the few really brilliant trees in the Island's autumn landscape. Even in winter, the young twigs and buds are reddish. As might

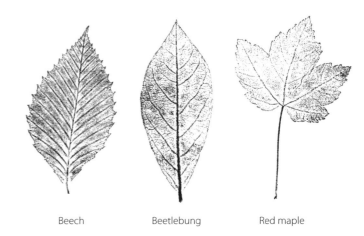

Beech   Beetlebung   Red maple

be expected, the blossoms in spring are crimson, as is the winged fruit that follows. The red maple is the only maple native to the Island.

Swamp azalea and sweet pepperbush are two common shrubs of wetland areas that grow here. To identify the swamp azalea, *Rhododendron viscosum*, look for a medium to tall shrub growing in the damp thickets beside the trail. Its simple leaves, without teeth, tend to cluster toward the end of the twigs. The very fragrant flowers—usually white though occasionally pink—bloom in summer.

Sweet pepperbush, *Clethra alnifolia*, is another shrub of swamps and wet places. Sometimes, particularly Up-Island, it grows in seemingly dry spots, which is usually a sign that a layer of clay is holding water close to the surface. Its habit of growth is upright, and its leaves are alternate, toothed, and short-pointed. The fragrant white flowers, which bloom in August, are small and clustered in short spikes.

In calm weather, observe the whirligig beetles spinning in circles on the surface of Ames Pond. Look, too, for water striders walking on top of the water, dimpling the surface with each step. Beneath the surface are diving beetles, perhaps still carrying a visible bubble of air, or deeper in the pond, water boatmen, like miniature upside-down rowers in tiny rowboats.

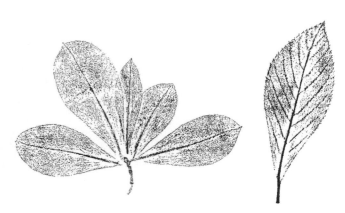

Swamp azalea

Sweet pepperbush

Whirligig beetles

Water boatman

In the vicinity of the pond lives *Pseudacris crucifer*, a frog called "pinkletink" on the Island. Elsewhere this diminutive frog is known as the spring peeper. The chorus of males vying with each other to attract a mate is the earliest and most welcome sound of spring.

Though they are numerous in freshwater wetlands in spring, and widely distributed over the eastern half of the country, pinkletinks can be an elusive bunch. Little is known of their habits outside of the breeding season when they are so conspicuously noisy. During that time, hundreds of them collect around slow, shallow water. At close range the males' high-pitched, two-note calls are shrill enough to make your ears ring. You may also hear the *gunk, gunk* call of the green frog.

To find a pinkletink in summer, try combing the ground in wet woodlands. Although they are members of the tree frog tribe and have discs on their feet, they don't climb trees to great heights, only about 40 inches up on vegetation. Look for a small frog, only about an inch, brown to pinkish in color with a dark cross, hence its name *crucifer*, on its back.

Before you leave Ames Pond, inspect the dam that was rebuilt in the mid-1970s by Mr. Ames. The original dam had boards that slipped in and out of a vertical slot. They were used to control the water level in what

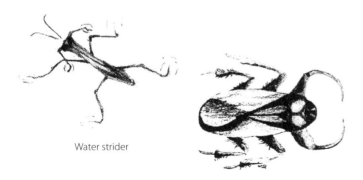

Water strider

Giant water bug

Pinkletink

was then a cranberry bog. A few cranberry plants still remain on the south side of the pond.

When you are ready to leave this idyllic spot, **turn away from the pond and follow the Yellow (Irons) Trail to the right**, which parallels the brook flowing from the dam at Ames Pond. On the right is a swampy area with more red maples and cinnamon ferns. Several kinds of mosses, in company with lichens, line the trail and cover the rocks. More and more ferns appear as the trail drops lower, a good place to try out the fern identification guide later in the book. **Follow the trail** through another beech grove and along a boardwalk. Nearby are several large rocks, or erratics.

Cross the stream on the wooden bridge. Continue to follow the trail, passing the Blue Trail that comes in from the left. At the intersection with the Purple Trail, which comes from the right, go left. About 30 paces ahead, look for a beech tree on the left side of the trail. Directly opposite and uphill a bit are three pygmy beeches that testify to the fierce and bitter winds that sweep through here in the winter. Since their upward growth is inhibited by the winter winds, the pygmies have used their energy to grow horizontally. The tree on the left, however, has been able to grow a bit taller because it is lower down on the slope and not as directly exposed to the shearing effect of the northwest wind that blasts the whole bluff above Daggett's Pond. Its top is on a level with the tops of the other pygmies. Possibly these trees are all the same age. Resist the urge to climb these trees. Keep them intact for the next generation of nature lovers to enjoy.

Continue along the Yellow Trail a short distance, past the intersection with the Red Trail on the right, which will take you back to the parking area when you are ready to return.

Once again **cross the brook** on another boardwalk. **Climb the sandy trail** that leads through the back dunes toward the beckoning beach. As you walk through the dune trail, notice the vegetation. Beach plum, beach grass, poison ivy, goldenrod, beach rose, and bayberry make their stand in the dunes, thriving even in this exposed habitat with its nutrient-poor soils.

Continuing on the trail to the beach, look for plants associated with the behind-the-dunes community, beach grass and beach heather or poverty grass, in particular.

Beach grass, *Ammophila breviligulata*, creeps up by underground stolons that help to stabilize dune areas. Inspect the structure of the grass using a hand lens if you have one. Looking closely at the upper side of the leaf, you can see parallel lines running from the tip of the leaf to its base—a feature of all grasses and other mono-cotyledons (flowering plants with one seed leaf). These are the veins of the plant positioned in a ribbed pattern to allow the leaf to roll easily and reduce its exposure to the dryness of its habitat. In this way, grasses ward off desiccation and can grow where little fresh water is available and endure the baking sun and drying winds.

Gently feel the sawtooth edges of the leaves. Obviously, animals would avoid grazing on these plants. Examine the base of the leaves for any salt crystals. Beach grass can process salt water and is able to exude the salt that it cannot use.

Beach heather, *Hudsonia tomentosa*, and its close relative *Hudsonia ericoides* are found in open sandy places throughout the Island. Because of its dense wooly hairs, *tomentosa* is especially suited to grow in exposed areas such as this part of the sanctuary.

The trail takes you to the ocean's edge and a beach where agates and a variety of other stones, glacial imports from the mainland, can be seen. There are quantities of boat shells, also called slipper snails, and to whet the appetite of any serious sheller, at least one rare Northern Cardita has been found along this beach. Enjoy the beachcombing as you go.

Walk along the shoreline to the right and take another right to get onto the Headland Loop Trail.

Be careful! Look around and among the trailside vegetation for poison ivy. If you don't already know it, now is a good time to become familiar with this very common plant. (See Tips for Trips, page 61.)

Poison ivy

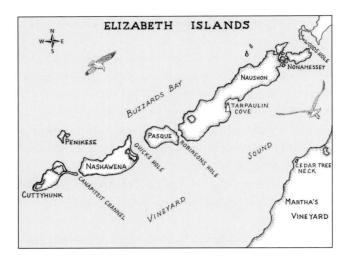

Several other plants may be confused with poison ivy. Brambles and blackberries also have three leaflets, but the leaf edges are regularly sawtooth and the whole plant is prickly, which you can see without touching. Another plant that often grows in association with poison ivy is the Virginia creeper—but it has five leaflets with tendrils for attaching itself and no aerial roots.

At the first intersection, **take a left and follow the trail up to the left to the overlook** for a spectacular view.

Across Vineyard Sound lie the Elizabeth Islands, and beyond, out of sight, Buzzard's Bay and the mainland.

Falmouth on Cape Cod can usually be seen to the northeast.

The Elizabeth Islands are privately owned, and access is prohibited except for a few locations, one of which is Tarpaulin Cove, located almost directly across the sound. A small lighthouse marks the southwesterly end of the lovely beach, which is a favorite picnic spot for the boating community.

From left to right, the first island is Cuttyhunk. Cuttyhunk contains the town of Gosnold, the governmental center of the Elizabeth Islands, which are part of the County of Dukes County, as is the Vineyard. Notice that it is not just "Dukes County." Confusion regarding this name has been used many times as a legal dodge.

The island of Nashawena lies close to Cuttyhunk, separated only by the narrow Canapitsit Channel, which is not visible from here. Between Nashawena and the next island, Pasque, is Quicks Hole, with a lovely sandy beach that is also popular with boaters. Robinsons Hole separates Pasque and Naushon, the largest and last of the big islands in the chain. Members of the extended Forbes family maintain homes on Naushon; some of their residences can be seen from Hadley Harbor at the northerly end of the island. One of the most popular harbors along the coast, Hadley offers good shelter and is delightfully picturesque. Woods Hole, with its notoriously swift currents, divides this island from the mainland.

After taking in the sights, **go back down to the Headlands and take a left to continue on the loop**. Other viewpoints are available on the left, but keep on the main trail to find yourself alongside Daggetts Pond. A species of short grass grows in the water close to the edge, and sweet gale lines the shore. This shrub is of the same genus as bayberry, *Myrica pensylvanica*. The leaves of sweet gale, *Myrica gale*, are similar to those of bayberry, but blue-green in color. The leaves of both shrubs are aromatic and were used for flavoring in colonial times.

The Headlands Loop Trail eventually takes you back to the beach. **Retrace your footsteps along the beach and take the Red Trail** (the one from which you emerged onto the beach) over the back dune, then into the woodland trail system where the **Yellow and Red Trails intersect**.

You now have the choice of a short or long route back to the parking lot. If you are in a hurry, **turn left to continue on the Red Trail**. In 10 minutes or less you will arrive at the parking lot.

For a longer walk and a spectacular view from the ridge, after you cross the brook, **take the Yellow (Bruce Irons) Trail to the Blue Trail (on the right). Follow the Blue Trail** along the ridge until it meets up with the White Trail. **Stay on the White Trail**, keeping your back to the water. This trail eventually takes you back to the original trailhead and parking lot. The timing of your arrival will depend on your pace, energy, and eagerness (or lack of it) to reenter the waiting world.

— **End of Trail** —

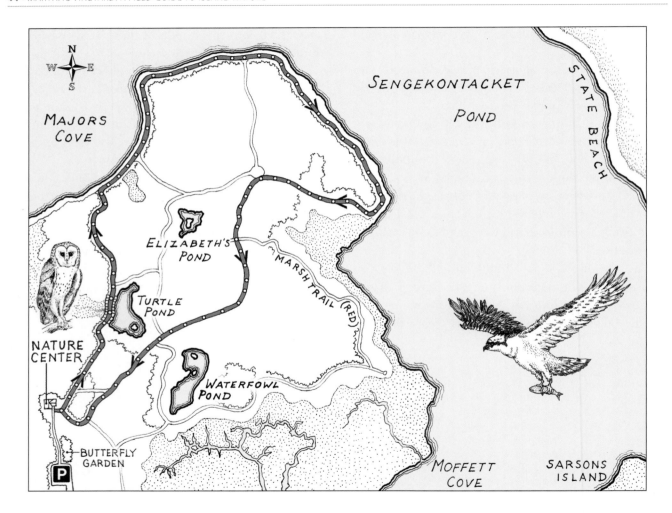

N W E S

MAJORS
COVE

SENGEKONTACKET

POND

STATE BEACH

ELIZABETH'S
POND

MARSH TRAIL (RED)

TURTLE
POND

NATURE
CENTER

WATERFOWL
POND

BUTTERFLY
GARDEN

P

MOFFETT
COVE

SARSONS
ISLAND

Mass Audubon's Felix Neck Wildlife Sanctuary

FAST FACTS

MAILING ADDRESS: PO Box 494 / Vineyard Haven, MA 02568 • **SITE ADDRESS:** 100 Felix Neck Drive / Edgartown, MA
CONTACT: 508.627.4850; felixneck@massaudubon.org • **OWNERSHIP:** Mass Audubon and Felix Neck Wildlife Trust (FNWT)
FEES: Mass Audubon members—Free, fee for nonmembers
NUMBER OF ACRES: 320 • www.massaudubon.org/felixneck

The place to go for nature education, the Discovery Room at Felix Neck's Nature Center has hands-on exhibits and live animals. Don't miss the barn owl cam, butterfly garden, and other opportunities to see Island wildlife.

Amenities: Nature Center with Discovery Room and Gift Shop, year-round restrooms, guided and self-guided kayak tours, educational programs and nature activities, summer day camp, four miles of trails, ample parking, public transportation (Bus Route 1) from Edgartown and Vineyard Haven. No bicycles on interior trails; no pets.

Directions: Felix Neck Wildlife Sanctuary is located off the Vineyard Haven–Edgartown Road. From the Triangle in Edgartown (the intersection where the roads to Oak Bluffs and Vineyard Haven split), the distance is 2.2 miles; coming from Vineyard Haven, the distance is 2 miles from the roundabout (formerly the blinker-light intersection and four-way stop) and 1 mile from County Road. A Mass Audubon sign and a boulder mark the entrance on the north side of the Vineyard Haven–Edgartown Road. Turn onto Felix Neck Drive, and drive the three-quarters of a mile to the sanctuary. Please accommodate other cars on this one-lane dirt road by using turnouts. Hikers and bikers should use the trail adjacent to the road for protection from dust and vehicles.

FELIX NECK Drive slowly and enjoy the ride into the sanctuary made more exceptional by the lack of overhead utility wires and the canopy of trees guiding your way. Immediately after turning onto Felix Neck Drive, look for the large, solitary boulder behind the Felix Neck sign. This rock is a ventifact (a stone shaped by the erosive action of windblown sand), unearthed when telephone and electric wires were laid.

The land on the right (east) side of the road is owned by the Martha's Vineyard Land Bank Commission, which purchased 25 acres in 2003. This acquisition assured that no houses would be built along this undeveloped stretch. You first pass through a zone of oak trees that gives way to pitch pines and then to an open field. Before Felix Neck became a sanctuary, the land had been farmed for generations, and the trees along the roadway show a common pattern of succession from field to forest that occurs when land is released from agriculture. The decrease in agriculture Island-wide has led to the natural conversion of land from fields to woodlands.

The areas that were most recently taken out of cultivation are dominated by pitch pines, while older, abandoned farm fields have succeeded to oak woodlands. A vista opens into large fields on both sides of the road. Here woodland succession is held back by annual mowing. Maintaining the open character of the land provides habitat for grassland birds, such as bobwhite and woodcock, and hunting grounds for raptors.

Osprey nesting platforms can be found on both sides of the field, although for many years only the one

Osprey

Barn owl

on the right has been occupied. Spring to late summer is the time to see the osprey family. Their progress can be observed starting with the female incubating her eggs, then the adults feeding the young, and finally the young can be seen preparing for flight. Females are differentiated from males by their larger size and the more pronounced "necklace" of dark brown feathers on their breast.

The tale of the ospreys' resurgence is a conservation success story. In 1964 there were only two nesting pairs of osprey on Martha's Vineyard. Long-term use of the chemical DDT had taken its toll on the species nationally, reducing the population's reproductive success. The chemical caused thinning of the birds' eggshells, which led to the eggs being crushed before they could hatch successfully. Ospreys also prefer to nest on tall trees, which allow them an expansive view of their surroundings. Large trees are not plentiful on the Vineyard because their growth is stunted by wind and salt spray, or they are cut down for firewood or blown down in storms.

Gus Ben David, Felix Neck's first director, began a program in which platforms on tall poles were installed across the Island to provide nesting areas for these birds. Though not all of them are used, more than 160 nesting platforms have been erected over the years, and the

> **"** It seems to me there is a real need for this organization [Felix Neck] to find means of bringing the story of conservation to the attention of more people. It is my feeling, and I hope yours, too, that this is the field in which we can contribute the greatest service to this Island. **"**
>
> —Anne Hale, 1964

osprey population has increased dramatically. In recent years, approximately 70 to 80 pairs of osprey breed successfully on the Island.

Small bird boxes in the field on the left provide nesting cavities for eastern bluebirds and tree swallows. The large rectangular box farther back (and after the Field Pond) houses barn owls, an uncommon bird in most of Massachusetts.

Park your vehicle in the dirt lot (bike racks are also available) and walk up the path to the Nature Center. The butterfly garden on your right should be explored after checking in at the Nature Center; its entrance faces the front of the Nature Center. Pick up a copy of the trail map and find out the latest wildlife sightings at the Nature Center before heading out on the trails. Spend some time in the Nature Center's Discovery Room, with its hands-on activities and barn owl cam that shares the antics of the building's avian inhabitants in real time.

The sanctuary is popular in all seasons and is a great resource for the community. Year-round nature education programs in the schools and community connect people and nature. Felix Neck's Fern and Feather Camp has been going strong for more than 50 years.

HISTORY Felix was a Wampanoag who lived on these lands in the first half of the 1600s. His full name was Felix Kuttashamaquat, which translates to "Felix His Neck." A neck is land that juts out into a body of water—in this case, Sengekontacket Pond. Wampanoags used Felix Neck for its natural resources, including plentiful shellfish and finfish and for hunting and gathering.

In 1664, Edgartown settlers divided the land at Felix Neck into 36 parcels that were distributed by the Edgartown Proprietors to those who were "cast or drawn." Island families including Pease, Norton, Daggett, Mayhew, and Smith were among those who acquired land at Felix Neck. These family names can still be found in the Island phone book, descendants of those early landholders.

By the late 1800s, almost all of the land at Felix Neck was owned by the Smith family. The Smiths worked and farmed this land for almost 300 years. Evidence of the Smith farmstead—including the foundations of two barns, a house, and a chicken coop—can still be found on the property today. The Nature Center was one of those barns.

George Moffett Jr. purchased Felix Neck in 1963 for $106,000 from Walter Smith, a descendant of the first Smith landowner. Both the Smith family and Moffett wanted the land protected forever.

The story of the Wildlife Sanctuary began in 1964 under the aegis of the Martha's Vineyard Natural History Society when Moffett gave the fledgling organization permission to use his newly acquired property to start a nature camp called Fern and Feather. In 1969 Gus Ben David was hired as the first sanctuary director, the name of the original organization was changed to the Felix Neck Wildlife Trust, and George Moffett began his generous donation of the property to Mass Audubon. Over the years, other parcels of land were donated or purchased, bringing the total amount of protected land on the Felix Neck peninsula to almost 350 acres.

NATURAL FEATURES The terrain seen from the Nature Center area is typical of the gently rolling land of the eastern section of the moraine. A variety of natural communities, wet and dry, can be found at this sanctuary.

Besides Sengekontacket Pond, the saltwater pond that surrounds the peninsula, freshwater and brackish ponds dot the property. All the ponds at the sanctuary were made by human hands except Bog Pond (formerly known as Old Pond) on the Jessica Hancock Memorial (Green) Trail, which is in a late stage in the progression of freshwater pond to woodland. It is believed that ice was once cut on this pond.

In the early years of the sanctuary, many wetland areas were dug out to create open-water habitat to attract wildlife, waterfowl in particular. Freshwater bogs, wet woodlands, and patches of open fields, as well as extensive woodlands of both oak and pine, thrive here. At one time, the expansive salt marsh could be seen from the Nature Center; however, as the woodlands have grown up, one must go to where the land meets the water to see the magnificent marshes.

TRAIL GUIDE

Start your walk by taking a left out the door of the Nature Center. Another left will put you on the Sassafras (Yellow) Trail. Keep the Nature Center on your left and walk straight down the trail, skirting the western edge of the fields. Examine the leaves on any oak tree or on the ground, and their variety is soon apparent.

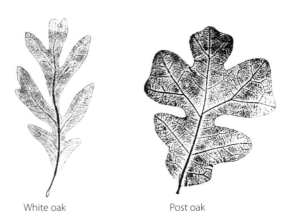

White oak   Post oak

Five oaks can be observed. Don't despair if you become confused as to their identity, as oaks tend to hybridize rather freely and their hybrids can confuse even the experts. Oak trees belong in either the white group, which has leaves with rounded lobes, or the black group, which has leaves with pointed lobes and bristles on the tips.

The white oak group here includes two species. White oak, *Quercus alba*, has fairly thin leaves and long, slender lobes nearly equal in size. Its bark is flaky and light in color. The post oak, *Quercus stellata*, has leaves that are thicker, more leathery, and often quite shiny, with unequal lobes. The upper two lobes, larger and often nearly square, look somewhat like ears.

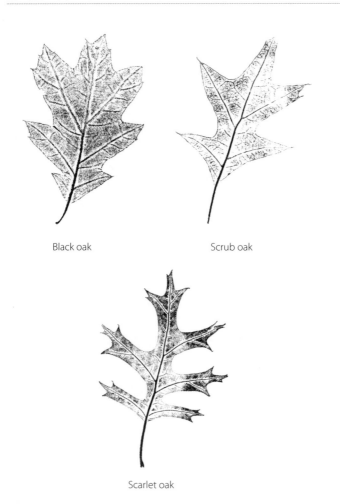

Black oak

Scrub oak

Scarlet oak

There are three members of the black oak group. The smallish scrub oak, *Quercus ilicifolia*, usually appears shrublike. Its small leaves with whitish undersides are beautifully shiny when the wind catches them. In shape they resemble holly leaves, as the species' botanical name indicates. The other two black oaks are differentiated by the comparative size of the lobes in relation to the sinuses (space between the lobes) of their leaves. The black oak, *Quercus velutina*, carries a solid leaf with shallow sinuses; the leaf of scarlet oak, *Quercus coccinea*, has a deep, well-rounded sinus and more slender lobes. These two species hybridize more frequently than others.

The fields on the right side of the Sassafras (Yellow) Trail are mowed to maintain the meadow. A few cedars have seeded in, but no pitch pine yet. Crabapple, pear, and other fruit trees were planted to provide food for wildlife.

The trail turns left into the woods and soon opens up to Turtle Pond. Excavated to provide freshwater habitat, salt water seeps in from the marsh and pond at high tides and during storms, making this pond slightly brackish (a mixture of salt and fresh water). However, turtles can still make their home here; look for painted or spotted turtles basking on rocks and logs on sunny summer days and snapping turtles laying eggs pondside.

Cross the Turtle Pond boardwalk. Take a left onto the Shad Trail. Sassafras trees and an understory of shadbush provide new interest on your route. Here you can identify the shrubs and trees by examining their bark.

The shadbush, *Amelanchier canadensis*, is known by its slender trunk with very smooth, striped gray bark patterned with lichen. The sassafras, *Sassafras albidum*, has deeply furrowed bark. Beetlebung, called tupelo, black, or sour gum off Island, has gray-brown bark, commonly in small, rectangular blocks. The bark of the white oak is flaky and light in color.

If unsure of the identification, look at the form of growth. Beetlebungs are distinguished by long branches growing almost horizontally from the trunk with short side branches. With their leaves down, they resemble spinning wood fairies, thus their scientific name, *Nyssa sylvatica*, which loosely translates to "nymph of the woods." The lengths of the side branches of the sassafras, white oak, and post oak are longer in comparison to the main branches. Those of the latter are more twisted. The branches of the sassafras come off of the trunk in a U shape, appearing to reach for the sky.

The shadbushes put on a memorable display in late April and early May. Drifts of white, five-petalled flowers spread below the leafless canopy of the taller trees. Another native shrub, the chokeberry, *Aronia melanocarpa*, blooms shortly after the shads. There are fewer

Snapping turtle

Shadbush

Chokeberry

chokeberries than shads on this trail, and they grow closer to the edge of the marsh. Their flowers are also white, but the petals are shorter.

The trail curves right, and shortly you will find yourself on the beach at Major's Cove. Major's Cove was named for Peter Norton, who was a major of the Dukes County Regiment in the 1760s. The houses across the water emphasize the sharp upswing in development throughout the Island. When the sanctuary was established, only one house could be seen at the head of the cove. As you walk out to the beach, be aware of the surrounding vegetation. Two types of shrubs line the inland edge of the narrow marsh that parallels the shore: marsh elder, *Iva frutescens*, and the groundsel bush, *Baccharis halimifolia*.

Differentiate them by their leafing pattern: opposite leafing for marsh elder, alternate leafing for groundsel bush. Compare the leaves to the accompanying prints. These two shrubs grow above all but the highest tides. In late autumn the white, fluffy flowers of the groundsel bush edge the marshes at Felix Neck.

Take a right and walk along the beach. The high-tide line is marked by a wrack line of mostly eelgrass, *Zostera marina*. As you stroll, look in the water and along the beach for shells, fish, crabs, and other marine life, but please leave these here for the next person to discover.

Boat shells or slipper snails, *Crepidula fornicata*, are common, and who wouldn't wonder about that scientific name? These shells stack up to reproduce; the larger ones on the bottom are female, and the smaller ones on top, male. As sequential hermaphrodites, their gender is changeable. The stack grows as more males land on top, and the males lower in the stack become female, never to change back.

Pick up a piece of eelgrass. It looks much like a single, long blade of blackened lawn grass. Many blades will be covered by minute left-handed white coils. These coils are marine worms known as sinistral spiral tubeworms, *Spirorbis borealis*. Eelgrass populations in Sengekontacket have suffered greatly due to disease and

Marsh elder   Groundsel bush

declining water quality. The loss of this species affects the common bay scallop, *Pecten irradians*, which uses the live grass growing in the pond as nursery habitat and protection from predators.

Perhaps the most exciting find will be a cast skeleton, or molt, of the horseshoe crab, *Limulus polyphemus*. To identify a molt, feel along the lower edge of the wide curve at the opposite end of the spiky tail. If it gives way under pressure, you are holding a molt. Observe the slit, which was the escape hatch for the little horseshoe crab, an arthropod that, like lobsters and true crabs, must cast off its shell to accommodate growth. Horseshoe crabs molt 20 times before they reach maturity. You will know if you have the remains of a dead crab

rather than a molt as the dead version is much less transparent and quite odiferous.

Horseshoe crabs are not true crabs—crustaceans—but members of the arachnid class that includes spiders and scorpions. They are among the oldest surviving fauna today, as their form has been virtually unchanged for 450 million years. Horseshoe crabs provide an important medical benefit; an extract from their blood is used to test for bacterial contamination of intravenous drugs and medical devices used

Common atlantic boat shell

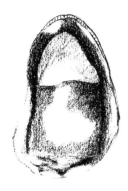

Eastern white boat shell

Bay scallops

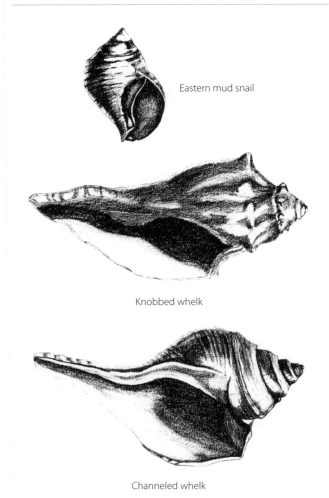

Eastern mud snail

Knobbed whelk

Channeled whelk

in the human body. During the high tides of May and June, horseshoe crabs come to the shores of Sengekontacket Pond and other locations to spawn.

In the water itself, if the tide is right, mud snails, *Nassarius obsolelus*, will be seen scattered over the bottom. Like an army of miniature aquatic vacuum cleaners, they eat the detritus (decaying organic matter) that lies on the floor of bays and lagoons. Mud snails deserve recognition for the important recycling role they play.

Pass by the Beach Trail, and continue along the shore around the point to the right, where you can see State Beach. Gulls regularly drop shellfish onto the rocky shoreline to crack them open so they can eat the animal inside. Judging by the shells on the beach, their favorite consists of large snails, known as whelks. Two species can usually be found: the channeled and knobbed whelks, *Busycon canaliculatum* and *Busycon carica*. Their names give a clue to their identification. A channel along the shell whorl distinguishes the channeled whelk; the knobbed whelk is knobby on the top of the whorl. The interior of fresh shells is colorful and shiny. Consider yourself lucky if you find a brown paisley-shaped operculum, the "trap door" of the whelk that protects the soft snail inside.

The beach is rockier here. This is a good place to look for ventifacts, small stones blasted by sand blown by high winds at the time the glacier lay nearby. This same force shaped the large boulder at the entrance to the sanctuary. Look for stones with flat, smooth facets with a rather sharp ridge between them. Most often the flat surfaces feel satiny smooth in contrast to the pronounced ridges—the "keels"—between the planes. These characteristics are often more easily detected by touch than sight.

You will soon come to the Sassafras (Yellow) Trail, whose bank has been greatly affected by erosion. **Pass by the Sassafras Trail and follow the shoreline around into the marsh where a narrow trail becomes apparent.** Though this trail can be wet, it offers spectacular marsh and beach views.

The richness and importance of marshes cannot be overemphasized. Each tide brings new nutrients to fertilize the marsh. Marshes serve as buffers to protect the more fragile areas behind. They also provide shelter and food for the young of most saltwater species that eventually find their way to your dinner table. Many kinds of fish, including bluefish and striped bass, rely on marshes during their life cycle. More than half of our country's marshes have been lost in the last 100 years.

Two marsh grasses can be seen here and at the edge of most salt marshes. Both are members of the same genus, *Spartina*. Identify them by the place where they grow, their texture, and their size. The taller, coarser plant, with its "feet" in the water most of the time, is cordgrass, *Spartina alterniflora*. *Spartina patens*, salt meadow grass, is the shorter, finer grass, farther away from the water and only reached by the highest of tides. Salt meadow grass, also called salt marsh hay, was once used as fodder for cattle, and in coffin mattresses, and still can be used as bedding for farm animals and mulch for gardens.

At the very edge of the marsh where the cordgrass grows, Atlantic ribbed mussels, *Modioilis demissus*, can be seen partially buried in the peat. Though these mussels are edible, consumption is not recommended, as

Atlantic ribbed mussel

they are tough and may cause stomach upset. They cannot begin to compare in taste with the blue mussel, *Mytilus edulis*, which grows in deeper and faster-moving water.

Once you reach the gray stones (brought in to line Waterfowl Pond), look for the Old Farm Road (Blue) Trail. Follow this trail until you reach the circle intersection. This was the location of the home of the last Smith family resident, Clarence, who lived a hermit's life at Felix Neck until his death.

Continue to your left and follow the Old Farm Road (Blue) Trail. This trail is wide because it was the road for the yellow buses that brought students to Felix Neck when the sanctuary first welcomed school groups. Elizabeth's Pond can be found down the wide trail on the right. Named for Elizabeth Goodale, former president of the Felix Neck Wildlife Trust, it is a nice side trip to see another of the property's freshwater ponds. **The Old Farm Road (Blue) Trail will take you back to the Nature Center directly; however, to lengthen your walk, take the Marsh (Red) Trail on your left.** If you follow the latter route, stop by Waterfowl Pond and look for the ducks, herons, and kingfishers that frequent the pond throughout the year.

Along the walk back on the Old Farm Road (Blue) Trail, appreciate the lichen on the trees. Lichens are symbiotic organisms comprising fungus and algae. They are considered pioneer species, establishing themselves where little else can grow and enriching the area to provide for other plants. To remember each part, think of this silly sentence, "Anna Algae took a 'lichen' to Fred Fungus, and the marriage is often on the rocks." You might see British soldiers, *Cladonia cristatella*, which can be easily identified by their red fruiting tips; pixie cups, *C. pyxidata*, which look like miniature green goblets; or reindeer moss, *Cladonia* species, which are not true mosses at all.

The fortunate may find earth stars, *Geasler hygrometricus*, a member of the mushroom family often associated with *Cladonia* lichens. A puffball tops each cluster of dark brown appendages that resemble stars in shape.

The Old Farm Road (Blue) Trail takes you back to the Nature Center area, passing by the backsides of both Waterfowl and Turtle Ponds, although they are harder to see when leaves create a dense barrier. Don't make this your only foray to Felix Neck. Visit in every season to see the changes in landscape, wildlife, and views.

— End of Trail —

|||||||||||||||||||||||||||||||||||||||||||||||||||||||||||||||||||||||||||||||||||||||||||||||||||||

**The forest was preserved to
save a now-extinct bird.**

|||||||||||||||||||||||||||||||||||||||||||||||||||||||||||||||||||||||||||||||||||||||||||||||||||||

Manuel Correllus State Forest

--- **FAST FACTS** ---

MAILING ADDRESS: PO Box 1612 / Vineyard Haven, MA 02568
SITE ADDRESS: State Forest Gate 18 along the Edgartown–West Tisbury Road
CONTACT: 508.693.2540; mass.parks@state.ma.us
OWNERSHIP: Massachusetts Department of Conservation and Recreation (DCR)
FEES: Free • **NUMBER OF ACRES:** 5,343 • www.mass.gov/dcr/parks/southeast/corr.htm
www.lostbirdproject.org/—The Lost Bird Project
www.mass.gov/dfwele/dfw/recreation/hunting/hunting_home.htm—Hunting information

The largest piece of conservation land on the Island provides incredible resources for recreation, though its history and role in the story of the extinction of the heath hen is perhaps its most compelling narrative.

Amenities: Bike paths, hiking, horseback riding trails, hunting, mountain biking, skiing (cross-country), walking trails. 14 miles of paved trails. Leashed dogs permitted. Free parking in many locations. Off-road vehicle use prohibited. Be aware of hunting seasons and wear blaze orange when appropriate. There are many points of entry to the State Forest, most of which are accessible by bus routes.

Directions: These directions are for the guided walk in this chapter that begins at Gate 18 in West Tisbury. Gate 18 is on the Edgartown–West Tisbury Road and can be found directly across from Deep Bottom Pond Road West. From Up-Island (West Tisbury, Chilmark, and Aquinnah), take the Edgartown–West Tisbury Road east toward Edgartown. Gate 18 is 1.75 miles from the start of the Edgartown–West Tisbury Road at the intersection of State Road in West Tisbury. It will be on your left as you head Down-Island; if you reach the airport entrance, you have gone too far. If you are starting from Vineyard Haven or Oak Bluffs, take

Barnes Road south to Edgartown–West Tisbury Road and go west (right). Those from Edgartown can follow the route from here. From the airport entrance, Gate 18 is 1.5 miles on the right. Parking is limited.

STATE FOREST Nestled in the center of the Island, the State Forest is notable for its size and recreational opportunities. Paved paths provide miles of car-free enjoyment for walkers, joggers, in-line skaters, and bicyclists. A Frisbee golf course, which begins at a parking area along Barnes Road, often draws a crowd.

You're likely to encounter few animals on a visit to the State Forest, though their tracks tell us of their presence. Many deer live throughout the State Forest, and their hoofprints can be found crossing the fire trails. Feral cats, offspring of stray cats that live here and multiply, are numerous and secretive. Raccoons and skunks live in the Forest, too, but they are generally active only at night. Owls inhabit these woods, and an evening visit may yield the calls of these night fliers.

You will definitely not meet the now-extinct heath hen, *Tympanuchus cupido cupido*, to which the State Forest owes its existence. When European settlers arrived on the East Coast, these birds were so abundant and easily hunted that servants negotiated with their employers to have to eat them only a few times per week!

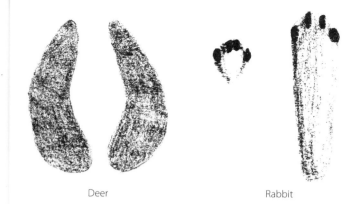

Deer

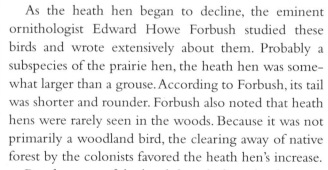

Rabbit

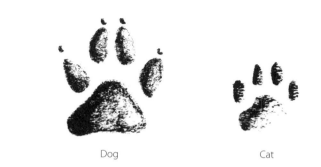

Dog   Cat

As the heath hen began to decline, the eminent ornithologist Edward Howe Forbush studied these birds and wrote extensively about them. Probably a subspecies of the prairie hen, the heath hen was somewhat larger than a grouse. According to Forbush, its tail was shorter and rounder. Forbush also noted that heath hens were rarely seen in the woods. Because it was not primarily a woodland bird, the clearing away of native forest by the colonists favored the heath hen's increase.

People aware of the heath hen decline closely monitored the number of birds and documented their findings. At times the population did increase, but in the end, even with protective legislation, the combination of overhunting; predation by foxes, raccoons, and

Courting heath hens by Louis Agassiz Fuertes

> ❝ And so it is that the extinction of the heath hen has taken away part of the magic of the Vineyard. There is a void in the April dawn, there is expectancy unanswered, a tryst not kept. Not until the great plain has grown again, a forest of tall pines and cedars, such as that which wooded the level acres a few centuries ago, will the loss of the heath hen be forgotten. ❞

—April 21, 1933, *Vineyard Gazette* editorial

hawks; loss of habitat; wildfires; very heavy rains at nesting time; and finally disease caused the heath hen to disappear forever. Manuel Correllus, former supervisor of the State Forest for nearly 60 years, may very well have been the last person to see a heath hen alive—in March 1932.

HISTORY The land in the middle of the Island was known as the "Great Plains" and thought of as worthless. As such, the center of the Island was for a long time undeveloped and lightly used. In 1698, one settler, a member of the Athearn family, called these lands "a barren ragged plain of no town." Another Islander, in 1794, identified it as "vast plains of bitter oaks between Edgartown and Tisbury."

In 1908 the State Forest was originally set aside in an effort to preserve the heath hen, a bird that had disappeared everywhere in the United States except on the Vineyard. Regrettably, the project was unsuccessful. The sole survivor of this species of birds, affectionately named "Booming Ben," was last seen on the Island in the early 1930s.

After the extinction of the heath hen, a forestation program was undertaken. The plantings were mainly red pines, *Pinus resinosa*. Some patches of white pine, *Pinus strobus*, and white spruce, *Picea glauca*, were added at intervals.

Today the State Forest provides for recreation, research, watershed protection, and open space.

NATURAL FEATURES The State Forest is the largest tract of contiguous conservation land on the Vineyard, totaling 5,343 acres. The entire parcel covers a good part of the outwash plain, the recharge area for the Island's water supply. The forest ground appears quite flat, but there are remnants of old meltwater streambeds from the glaciers. Exploration with a topographic map shows some rather steep slopes, which can be seen along selected trails.

The meltwater streambeds are called frost bottoms, and a microclimate is associated with them. Cold air

TIPS FOR TRIPS

POISONOUS PLANTS: Poison ivy grows abundantly and luxuriantly on the Island in many habitats and forms.

It is most widespread in areas where land has been disturbed, but you can find it in sand dunes and woodlands as ground cover, shrubs, and even as small trees. The leaves tend to be shiny in sunshine, dull in shade, and are somewhat variable in shape.

Just remember that poison ivy is the only thornless, alternate-leaved woody plant with three leaflets on a long leaf stalk that you will find on the Island. Usually you can see light tan buds in the axils of the leaves and at the tips of the branches. Often whiskery-looking aerial roots are seen along the stems.

A second plant that can cause a toxic reaction is poison sumac. Contact with this plant is unlikely if you stay on the trails, as there are relatively few poison sumacs on the Vineyard, and they usually grow in wet places where waterproof boots are needed. The chances of contacting poison sumac are slim, but learn to recognize it anyway.

Poison sumac is quite different in appearance from poison ivy. It is a tall shrub also with compound leaves, but each leaf has seven to nine leaflets, versus the three for poison ivy. Both plants have white, berrylike fruits.

(Poison oak, a third plant that can cause a toxic reaction, is not indigenous to the Vineyard.)

A GOOD RULE OF THUMB: LOOK FOR LEAFLETS THREE AND LEAVE IT BE.

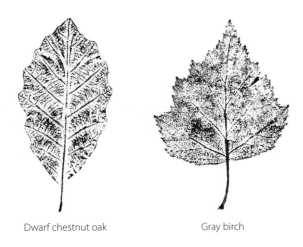

Dwarf chestnut oak   Gray birch

drains from the higher lands of the forest into and through them to the sea, just as the glacial meltwater once did. The dominant plant species in the frost bottoms is the hardy scrub oak, *Quercus ilicifolia*, which, unlike most other plants, can survive the frosts that sometimes blacken and kill the first spring growth. It is not unusual to be able to feel the temperature differences during a walk or bicycle ride on the hilly bike path along the Edgartown–West Tisbury Road. Frost has occurred in these bottoms in every month of the year.

On the higher elevations, the post oak, *Quercus stellata*, is seen in great numbers standing tall above the scrub oaks. Its scruffy, white bark and drooping, twisted limbs give it a scarecrow-like appearance. Its leaf has rounded lobes; the upper two, larger than the others, look a bit like big ears.

The landscapes of the State Forest, although superficially similar, display considerable variety when explored closely. You will find stands of introduced tall red pines, with thick carpets of needles beneath. Needles of the red pine are found bound in groups of two, which contrast to pitch pine and white pine, whose needles are found in groups of three and five, respectively. The forest is in a late stage of succession to woodlands. Gone are the open, scrubby heathlands that were characteristic years ago, when repeated fires slowed succession and retained the preferred habitat of the heath hen.

The red pine is a boreal (more northern) tree, and the Vineyard is beyond the limit of its natural range. Any species on the outer edge of its range is under constant stress and is more susceptible to disease and insect infestation. Unfortunately, so much of the forest was planted with red pine that it technically became a monoculture.

An infection caused by the fungus *Diplodia pinea* is killing the pines. Once an infestation starts in a monoculture it spreads quickly and is almost impossible to control. Dead and dying pines are still visible. The white pine, *Pinus strobus*, and white spruce, *Picea glauca*, have survived and are reproducing well, a sign of their acclimation to the area.

Red cedars, *Juniperus virginiana*, are seldom seen. On some of the higher elevations, pitch pines, *Pinus rigida*, still dominate. The oak genus, or tree group, Quercus, is well represented and includes the dwarf chestnut oak, *Quercus prinoides*, as well as the more common oaks. Gray birch, *Betula populifolia*; bigtooth aspen, *Populus grandidentata*; quaking aspen, *Populus tremuloides*; and a gray willow, *Salix cinerea*, grow here, too.

Heath hen memorial stone

TRAIL GUIDE

Park at Gate 18 and start your visit at the Heath Hen Memorial Stone through the metal gate and on the left nestled up against the woodland. Toy birds left behind demonstrate Islanders' affection for this long lost, but not forgotten, Vineyard resident.

Begin your walk by keeping the memorial on your left and heading north (straight ahead). Shortly you will see, through some trees, an open field on your left.

Continue, following the paved trail. Alongside the pavement, low creeping plants are the norm as repeated mowing maintains the current condition of plant growth. The thick, hairy leaves of the mayflowers, *Epigaea repens*, can be found on the ground for most of the year. It is no surprise that its scientific name translates to "creeping upon the earth." Also known as trailing arbutus, its small, white flowers are one of the first seen in spring.

Wintergreen, *Gaultheria procumbens*, also commands attention in its low-down locale, especially because of its thick, green leaves and red berries that brighten (and flavor) even the grayest winter day. Scented waxy leaves of this plant (also known as teaberry, checkerberry, boxberry, and partridgeberry) are edible, as are its red berries, which historically have been used to flavor chewing gum, wine, and teas. Micro shrub bearberry, *Arctostaphylos uva-ursi*, mixes in with the lowlife.

Stop when you get to Marker 4E, where the paved trail turns sharply left. Straight ahead the fire lane continues north. To get off the beaten path, look diagonally (to the left) between the fire lane and the paved trail for a narrow unpaved trail that heads into the woods. Follow it, leaving the blacktop behind.

As you walk along, note that the trail heads downward. This low area is part of the Willow Tree Frost Bottom. Frost bottoms, with their unique geologic formation and resultant conditions, host more than a few rare species, especially moths. Cold gathers in the bottoms at night, but by day the lack of trees keeps temperatures high. A variation of 70 degrees in one day is possible in a frost bottom.

Coming upon white spruce groves feels strangely un-Vineyard-like. Along with the red pines, these groves were planted for commercial purposes at various times in the Forest's history. One such planting was undertaken by the Civilian Conservation Corps (CCC), also known as "Roosevelt's Tree Army," during the Great Depression. In contrast to the red pines, the spruce are surviving and reproducing. Lichen covers many of the trees, having clearly taken a liking to them, too.

The fire lanes open up the landscape. This rectangular grid system of unpaved lanes was originally established to provide fire breaks for the protection of heath hens whose numbers greatly declined after wildfires spread across the forest. In the 1930s the *Vineyard Gazette* noted that "hardly a spring passes that does not see a fire started somewhere on the plains." Half-square-mile blocks are delineated with 50-foot fire lanes between them. With the property's massive size, it might seem easy to get lost in the State Forest; however, these fire lanes can help you navigate once you know the system. North/South lanes are numbered and East/West lanes are lettered. Intersections often have markers to keep you oriented.

Thus, many options exist to lengthen or shorten walks in the State Forest with its more than 30 miles of roads and firebreaks. **For a shorter route, take a left when you reach the first fire break (fire lane D) and walk the fire lane until you get to intersection 3D (several hills away). Then take another left onto fire lane 3 and walk until you reach the paved trail. For a longer option, cross over the first fire lane (D), continue on the narrow trail through the woods**

until you reach the second fire lane (C). Take the next two left turns and you will be back on track on fire lane 3 heading south.

When standing in the middle of the fire lanes and looking at the expansive view ahead of and behind you, it is easy to imagine this landscape open and unforested in times past.

Walking south along fire lane 3 takes you back to the paved path, though stop to appreciate the enormity and unrestrained feeling of the landscape. When you reach the paved bike path, a granite marker and the word "slow" on the bike path confirm

your location. **However, you can continue on a foot path that parallels the paved trail for more interesting sights. On the left before the pavement is a narrow dirt trail; take it and keep hidden from the hustle and bustle of the blacktop path and road beyond.**

An old wooden sign on a pitch pine tree on the right of the trailhead identifies it. The MVRHS (Martha's Vineyard Regional High School) Horticulture Puckerbrush Path "welcomes equestrians and walkers." This trail was laid in the early 1980s. Along the narrow trail, posts remain from a scientific study designed to determine the effects of fire behavior on various woodland fuels. The number of the post indicates which plot it is, and the letters describe the forest type and treatment. For example, PP identifies pitch pine, OW for oak woodland, SO indicates scrub oak, G is where grazing occurred, B is where fuels were burned, and C is where cutting was the treatment. Lastly, the large area that looks burned is just that. The experiment generated lots of limbs that needed to be disposed of before State Forest officials were able to set fire to the test plots.

This dirt trail eventually connects with the paved bike path, which brings you to the last standing heath hen. This imposing figure was sculpted by artist Todd McGrain, as part of his Lost Bird Project, which "recognizes the tragedy of modern extinction by immortalizing North American birds that have been driven to extinction." This sculpture is a tribute to this bird's past glory and a reminder of what we have lost.

Follow the paved trail (around marker 4E) and turn right to return to your car at Gate 18. Plan to come back to the State Forest often to explore further the miles of trails. Come in April to find the first mayflowers; in May to see the birds-foot violets, *Viola pedata*; and in June for lady's slipper orchids, *Cypripedium acaule*. And when thinking of the State Forest, always remember the heath hen, for as Todd McGrain said, "Forgetting is another kind of extinction."

— End of Trail-

Todd McGrain's heath hen sculpture

Long Point Wildlife Refuge

FAST FACTS

MAILING ADDRESS: PO Box 2106 / Vineyard Haven, MA 02568

SITE ADDRESS: Off the Edgartown–West Tisbury Road / West Tisbury, MA

MID-JUNE TO MID-SEPTEMBER: Hughe's Thumb Road entrance • **MID-SEPTEMBER TO MID-JUNE:** Thumb Point Road entrance

CONTACT: 508.693.3678; longpoint@ttor.org • **OWNERSHIP:** The Trustees of Reservations

FEES: Summer entrance, mid-June to mid-September: Trustees: Free admission, parking fee. Nonmembers: Fee per person and parking fee. Off-Season entrance, mid-September to mid-June: free to all.

NUMBER OF ACRES: 632 • www.thetrustees.org

When the Island's wild south shore beckons, Long Point is the perfect response. Buffeted by coastal salt ponds and edged by the ocean, it is easy to see the beauty that led city folks here for the respite and relaxation offered at this former hunting club.

Amenities: Mountain biking is permitted only on designated trails. Horseback riding is prohibited. Swimming may be hazardous due to rough surf and undertows. There are no lifeguards on duty; swim at your own risk. There are no trash receptacles. Please carry out what you carry in. Trail and beach wheelchair available. Seasonal hunting (waterfowl only) is permitted at this property subject to all state and town laws. In addition, a Trustees of Reservations permit is required to hunt.

Directions: There are two different entrances for Long Point Wildlife Refuge, depending on the season. Summer visitors go for the beach and swimming options, and the parking lot fills quickly on sunny days. Both entrance roads are long and bumpy, so take care and drive slowly. The guided walk described here begins at the off-season property entrance.

Access: Mid-June through mid-September:

Entrance is from Edgartown–West Tisbury Road, about 0.3 miles west of the main entrance to the airport. Turn onto Waldron's Bottom Road and follow for 1.3 miles. Turn left onto Scrubby Neck Road (Path), then right onto Hughe's Thumb Road, and follow signs for 1.2 miles to summer parking area. Plan to visit early in the day, particularly on sunny weekends in midsummer; visitors are turned away when the parking lot is full.

Access: Mid-September through mid-June:

Entrance is from Edgartown–West Tisbury Road, about 1.1 miles west of the main entrance to airport. Turn onto Deep Bottom Road and follow for 1.5 miles, always bearing left at forks. Turn right onto Thumb Point Road and follow for 1.3 miles to off-season parking area.

LONG POINT Long Point Wildlife Refuge encompasses 632 acres of woodlands, pond, moorland, and almost half a mile of south shore beach. The variety of habitat, particularly the coves with both fresh and salt water, attracts waterfowl to the area and, during migration, shorebirds.

The refuge is notable for its large concentration of rare species, which includes more than 30 animals and 11 plants. Piping plovers, short-eared and snowy owls,

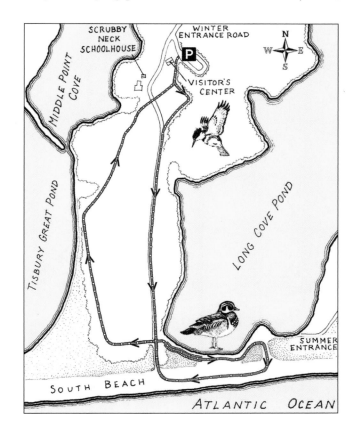

Snowy owl, a recent winter visitor

and a few species of moths top the animals list, while special species of plants include seabeach knotweed, *Polygonum glaucum*; Nantucket shadbush, *Amelanchier nantucketensis*; bushy rockrose, *Helianthemum dumosum*; sandplain blue-eyed grass, *Sisyrinchium fuscatum*; and sandplain flax, *Linum intercursum*.

HISTORY Plentiful resources on land and water provided for Native American settlements that were likely more dense at Long Point than other areas of the Island. Wampanoag place names provide history and context. Seconquit, Pasquanahommon's Neck, Takemmy, Mussoowonkwonk, and Wachepemepquah are original place names that describe the people and activities of the time. Pasquanahommon, for example, was a sachem of Tisbury, and Wachepemepquah is translated as "planting field" or "cornfield," describing the area as agricultural during presettlement times.

Later, colonists farmed the land, and early deeds mention the dwellings and outbuildings, some of which remain today. Until 1889 Scrubby Neck School operated at Long Point, and the former school building still exists on the property.

During the first half of the 1900s, Long Point was renowned as one of the best water-fowling areas on the Vineyard. For many years, the property was owned by

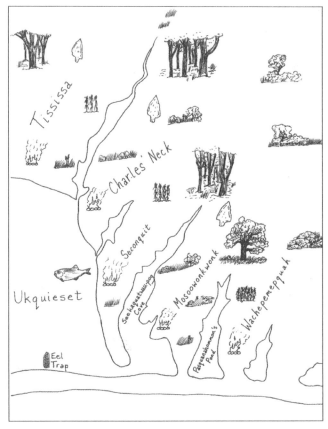

Rendition of Long Point in 1671, showing place names, native settlements (fires), hunting grounds (arrowheads), agricultural areas (corn), and various habitats ranging from grasslands to Scrub Oak shrublands.

a private group, the Tisbury Pond Club, and used for hunting. The former Tisbury Pond Clubhouse is now a residence.

The Trustees of Reservations acquired Long Point in 1979, and the refuge is used for educational purposes, surf fishing, bathing, and picnicking, while providing habitat for wildlife and an abundance of rare species.

NATURAL FEATURES Extending to the ocean edge of the outwash plain at South Beach, Long Point borders Tisbury Great Pond and Middle Point Cove to the west and surrounds Long Cove Pond on the east. These ponds resulted from the flooded meltwater streams of the Wisconsin glaciations period.

Many plant communities of the Vineyard are represented on the refuge. Oak woodlands, including a 30-acre tract of oak-hickory, are found near the parking lot. Pitch pine, *Pinus rigida*, and scrub oak, *Quercus ilicifolia*, dominate the northern portion of the refuge. At Long Cove Pond, the woodlands open into an old field-shrub community; huckleberry thickets and grasslands cover other areas. Approaching the beach, the open moor-like character of the land results from a history of grazing; the frequent harsh, salt-laden winds that sweep in from the Atlantic Ocean; and the effect of fires.

Tisbury pond clubhouse

The water of Long Cove Pond, as in most of the great ponds, is fresh near its head, the northern end, and sometimes brackish nearer the outer beach. Freshwater streams flow into Tisbury Great Pond, and elsewhere fresh water seeps out from the water table. The salinity of these ponds varies individually and seasonally. Severe storms can break through the south shore barrier beach, and often the ponds are opened artificially. At Tisbury Great Pond, from at least 1715 to the current day, periodic breaches in the barrier beach have been made to maintain the lowland meadows, accommodate the migrations of fish, sustain shellfish resources, prevent flooded cellars, and for swimming, crabbing, and harboring boats.

TRAIL GUIDE

Use the **off-season entrance (mid-September– mid-June)** for this guided walk or join the trail from the summer side entrance at Long Cove Pond. **From the parking lot, take the trail toward the Visitor Center** and read the bulletin board, grabbing a map if needed. **Walk through the woods, toward the sound of the surf,** noticing how quickly the trees shorten in height, sculpted and kept low by the winds and salt spray. **At the trail intersection, take the left trail** and immediately look for a few pignut hickory trees, *Carya glabra*, growing at the edge of the woodlands. In the winter, their round, bulbous buds and heart-shaped leaf scars give them away. On the right are bluebird boxes, often used by the tree swallows that dart about in the open field. **Follow the trail to the right** to take you toward the open field. **A left turn at the intersecting trail** leads to the ocean beach.

Tree swallow

" O Lord, from errors' ways defend us lest we mistake thy will for luck. Give us, at dawn, a flight stupendous. Don't send us coot, but geese and duck. **"**

—Saying grace at the Tisbury Pond Hunting Club, circa early 1900s (from the Tisbury Pond Club logbook)

Before you reach the dune, a boardwalk on your left at the bottom of Long Cove beckons. It invites you to skirt around the southern edge of this coastal salt pond, taking you to the Island's south shore and ocean interface.

Coastal salt ponds are unique, formed by glacial action and the water flooding out of the outwash plain. Dammed by the south shore barrier beach and fed fresh water though streams and groundwater, these ponds have varying rates of salinity, depending on ocean overwash and the opening of the pond by storms or human hands. The boardwalk leads you to the southern tip of Long Cove Pond and its interface with the powerful sea.

At the end of the boardwalk go to the ocean and take a right, walking west along the ocean shoreline to appreciate the true magic of the Long Point beach. Keep an eye out for the trail on the right, which leads back to the field.

The beach, which on a map looks like a long, smooth crescent, takes on a different aspect when viewed at close range from its edge. Waves brushing against the beach at an angle leave it cusped and scalloped. The prevailing easterly movement of the water, a *littoral current*, works with the waves to move the sand along the beach grain by grain, gently or swiftly depending on conditions. Here, littoral currents usually move to the east. The sand beneath your feet at Long Point may have been in the Lucy Vincent Cliffs in Chilmark last year. Over time, it will have traveled down the shore, perhaps continuing to South Beach in Edgartown.

If only it were possible to tag one grain of sand and follow its voyage from day to day, season to season, year after year. Where will the grain be found next spring or a century from now? Wasque? Beneath the waves offshore under a school of feeding bluefish? Eventually part of a rock again? During all the time they are within reach of the waves, sand grains waltz along in an easterly direction, spiraling around and around along other beachfronts touched by the ocean currents.

The beach itself, along with the ocean, is in great flux. Ocean waves constantly alter its edges, rearrange its components, and reshape its contours. In winter, the beach shortens and becomes steeper; in summer, it flattens out again. The Vineyard's South Shore is known for this dynamic behavior; on average, four to six feet of beach can be lost annually.

Pick up a handful of sand and look closely at the variety of shapes and colors. While most sand particles are rounded, clear or whitish-beige grains of hard, enduring quartz, others are chunky pink, tan, or gray bits of feldspar. Some darker particles perhaps are magnetite, an iron compound that, as its name suggests, responds to a magnet. You may also see green-black grains of hornblende, flakes of mica, little dots of pink or red garnet, bits of round grains of green olivine—all common minerals that compose sand. Other minerals that may be seen include flecks of amber or amethyst; green or black particles may be tourmaline; beryl and sapphire and topaz may also appear. The numbers are numbing when you contemplate the multitude of grains of sand or even just the few under foot.

Below the wave-washed sand live animals particularly adapted to take advantage of this difficult environment. No sign of life might be seen except the air holes of the creatures below where they take shelter between the tides, waiting for the returning waves to bring them their next meal. Higher up the beach, you may find one of their telltale shells. Look for a stream-lined shell about an inch long, pale grayish-tan in color. It is an Atlantic mole crab, *Emerita talpoida*. Mole crabs

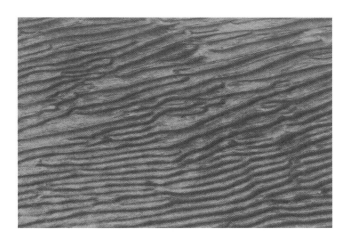

Surf clam   Chestnut astartes   Transverse arks

are well-designed for living under the sand and for bur-rowing quickly beneath the surface to seek shelter. A recently arrived resident hailing from more southern shores is the Atlantic ghost crab, whose deep burrows can sometimes be seen on the beach.

The high-tide line, or wrack line, deserves explora-tion. The shells of species found deeper in the ocean might be seen. Discover surf clams, *Spisula solidis-sima*; chestnut astartes, *Astarte castanea*; transverse arks, *Anadara transversa*; and if you're really lucky, the brown paisley-shaped operculum, or trap door, of a whelk, left behind by the force of the ocean waves.

Kelp and Irish moss are seaweeds often spread along the wrack line. If lifted aside, sand fleas or beach-hop-pers will jump away. The strange black egg case of the skate, *Raja erinacea*, and pieces of driftwood festooned with gooseneck barnacles, *Lepas fascicularis*, might also be found.

Leave the beach and return to the open fields by way of the first established path through the dune. Take a minute to admire the dunes; those protectors of the coast need protection themselves to do their job. Look at but don't touch the plant life on the sidelines, including poison ivy, which in turn holds the dunes in place. Beach grass, *Ammophila breviligulata*, is most obvious, but you can find the silver fuzzy leaves of dusty miller, *Artemisia stelleriana*; purple blossoms of beach pea, *Lathyrus japonicus*; and handsome seaside goldenrod, *Solidago sempervirens*, there, too.

Make your walk a loop by following the trail to the left and around the field. Before you, Tisbury Great Pond shows its grandeur. On clear days, notice the sandy barrier beach beyond the pond that separates the pond from the ocean. Though nat-ural and human-induced pond breaches occurred earlier, since the 1900s, its opening was mandated by "An Act to Provide Drainage of the Lowlands and Meadows around Certain Great Ponds in the County of Dukes County." Elected officials called "sewers" are still responsible for deciding the frequency of the pond's opening.

In the open fields on your right, look for these sandplain grassland species: Eastern blue-eyed grass, *Sisyrinchium atlanticum*; pineweed or orange grass, *Hypericum gentianoides*; frostweed or rockrose, *Helianthemum* species; and lowbush blueberry, Vaccinium species. Vegetation in the field contains stands of grass, mainly little bluestem, *Schizachyrium scoparium*, with a mixture of wildflowers. Find Pennsylvania sedge, *Carex pensylvanica*, with its triangular stems; sand jointweed, *Polygonella articulata*; thistles, *Cirsium* species; and sweet fern, *Comptonia peregrina*. In the late summer and early fall, when the little bluestem turns blush color, it makes a particularly beautiful foil for the many wildflowers that grow in this field.

Eastern blue-eyed grass

Out in the open field, on the edge of Middle Point Cove to the west, you will see the old Tisbury Pond Clubhouse and smaller Scrubby Neck Schoolhouse, which, at its busiest, boasted 14 students.

Follow signs to the parking lot and enjoy Ben Cabot's stone bird sculpture along the way. Another time, be sure to return to explore Long Point's woodlands and the upper ends of the coves of Tisbury Great Pond.

— **End of Trail** —

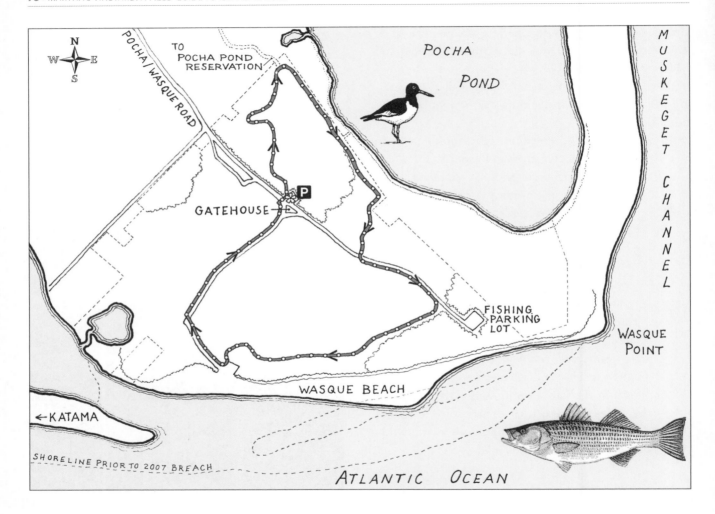

N
W · E
S

TO
POCHA POND
RESERVATION

POCHA/WASQUE ROAD

POCHA
POND

MUSKEGET CHANNEL

P

GATEHOUSE

FISHING
PARKING
LOT

WASQUE
POINT

WASQUE BEACH

← KATAMA

SHORELINE PRIOR TO 2007 BREACH

ATLANTIC OCEAN

||||||||||||||||||||||||||||||||||||||||||||||||||||||||||||||||||||||||||||||||||||||||||||||||||||||||

Change is the only constant at Wasque.

||||||||||||||||||||||||||||||||||||||||||||||||||||||||||||||||||||||||||||||||||||||||||||||||||||||||

Wasque Reservation

---- **FAST FACTS** ----

MAILING ADDRESS: PO Box 2106 / Vineyard Haven, MA 02568

SITE ADDRESS: Wasque Road / Chappaquiddick, Edgartown, MA

CONTACT: 508.627.6789 / Tour Line 508.627.3599 / capepoge@ttor.org • **OWNERSHIP:** The Trustees of Reservations

FEES: Memorial Day weekend through Columbus Day weekend: Trustees members:
Free. Nonmembers: Fee per person and parking fee. Allow a minimum of one and a half
hours, longer if also visiting other Chappaquiddick conservation properties.

NUMBER OF ACRES: 200 • www.thetrustees.org

Located on the island of Chappaquiddick, Wasque is a place defined by the force of the ocean and the whims of storms. Over the last few years, it has been hard hit by erosion.

Amenities: Public restrooms and picnic areas available. Dogs must be kept on a leash at all times. Bikes are permitted on trails only—not on the beach. Depending on conditions, oversand vehicle access to Wasque via The Trustees' Cape Poge Wildlife Refuge may be possible. Swimming and walking conditions can change dramatically due to conditions resulting from periodic breaches at Norton Point Beach. For the latest conditions and advisories, go to The Trustees of Reservation website or call the Gatehouses. Two other Trustees properties, Mytoi and Cape Poge, add to any Chappaquiddick itinerary; guided tours are offered seasonally. The Martha's Vineyard Land Bank also has properties to explore on Chappaquiddick.

Directions: To visit Wasque Reservation, take the Chappy Ferry from Edgartown to Chappaquiddick.

❝ The most beautiful place in the world. **❞**

—Edo Potter, longtime Chappaquiddick resident

The Chappy Ferry is located at 53 Dock Street in Edgartown, and vehicles, walkers, and bicycles can board here. The vehicle waiting line forms on Daggett Street; when busy, the line can extend back onto Simpson's Lane, and waiting time can exceed one hour. Once on Chappaquiddick, follow the paved road to the end and continue along the dirt road into the reservation. This trail guide walk begins at the parking lot on the left just past the first gatehouse.

WASQUE Even on Chappaquiddick, known as "the separate island," Wasque really is the end of the line. The road through the reservation ends abruptly at a cliff at the water's edge. In fact, the word "Wasque" (pronounced "way-skwee") is derived from an Algonquin word, "wannasque" meaning "the ending point."

Wasque has been defined by its history of dramatic landscape change. Chappaquiddick has been both a peninsula, attached to the rest of Martha's Vineyard by a barrier beach, or an island, when the ocean breaches the connecting land. A breach happens regularly and somewhat predictably, occurring intentionally by human hands and, more often, naturally. Since 1775, at least

12 breaches have been recorded. On average, breaches occur every 20 to 30 years and stay open usually from 13 to 17 years. The most recent breach at Norton Point (the connecting barrier beach) occurred in April 2007, 16 years after a brief opening that resulted from Hurricane Bob and 40 years after the last long-lived breach.

HISTORY The Native Americans that first inhabited these lands were Wampanoag and called themselves Chappaquiddicks. These were the first humans to live on the Vineyard, beginning more than 10,000 years ago. There is evidence that the Wampanoag first walked to the Island by coming north along the wide coastal plain, tracking mammoths and mastodons while the sea still lay farther away. They occupied settlements near the beach in summer, inland in winter. Native American middens, their trash dumps, show that besides the animals they hunted, their menu included plants gathered on shore and fish and shellfish extracted from the sea. Many of the earliest campsites were buried beneath the ocean as sea levels rose in the postglacial period.

In the early 1600s the first colonists arrived and bought land from the Wampanoag on Chappaquiddick. For almost 200 years these Edgartownians used the Chappy fields as winter pastures for sheep and cattle but did not build permanent structures, choosing to

Typical migration of opening into Katama Bay

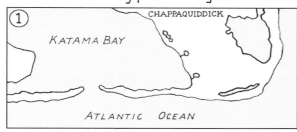

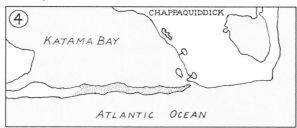

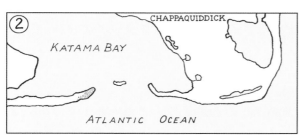

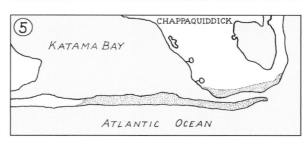

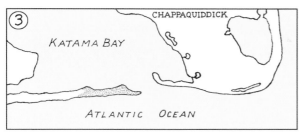

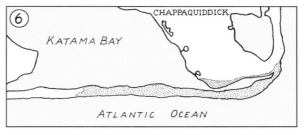

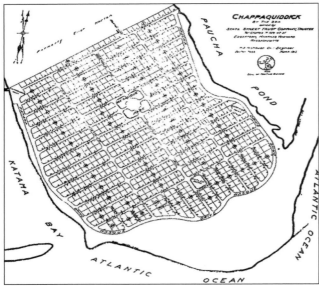

A planned, but never built subdivision.

live on the main island instead. Livestock were walked over in October to graze Chappaquiddick's uplands and would return in April to the bigger island.

Island fishermen and farmers began to settle on Chappaquiddick in the mid-1750s. With the growth of the whaling industry, the population rose, and by 1878 the residents included many whaling captains living on Chappy year-round. Today, the population of Chappaquiddick is about 150 hearty year-round

residents. An exact accounting of seasonal residents is difficult, though anecdotal information suggests that likely more than 3,000 people call this island home in the summer months.

During the late 19th century, development schemes were planned for the separate isle. Inviting names, such as Wasque Farms, Chappaquiddick-by-the-Sea, and Country Club Estates, described summer fun and fancy, offering 50-by-100-foot lots for seaside dream homes. Fortunately, none of these subdivisions were built. Conservation came to Wasque in 1967, when a determined group of Chappaquiddick residents raised $250,000 to purchase the property.

NATURAL FEATURES Wasque Point reaches out farther toward Nantucket than any other part of the Vineyard. In clear weather, it is possible from the bluffs along the beach to see Muskeget Island, Tuckernuck Island, and Nantucket, the last of which is about 19 miles away from Wasque. Even further, consider the trip all the way to Portugal, which lies about 3,000 miles across the Atlantic on the same latitude.

The southwest corner of the Vineyard, including Chappaquiddick, is composed of morainal deposits from the Cape Cod lobe of the Wisconsin glacier that were later covered with outwash from the Buzzard's

Bay lobe. The highest point on Chappy is Sampson Hill, with an elevation of 94 feet above sea level.

Chappaquiddick is normally connected to the Vineyard by a spit of land extending to South Beach, Edgartown, via Norton Point at Katama. Chappy becomes an entirely separate island when severe storms and high tides break through the barrier beach. The beaches of the bar linking Chappaquiddick to Katama turn north from Wasque Point and stretch to Cape Poge, and are among the Vineyard's most dramatic landforms.

It is difficult to imagine the wildness of winter storms and hurricanes here, or the damage that they inflict on the land. However, a long history of breaches in the beach have cut through and connected the ocean to Katama Bay.

During violent weather in 1856, 1886, 1938, 1954, and 2007, breaches took place in about the same location on the westerly end of the beach at Norton Point. The record of these breaches reveals a predictable

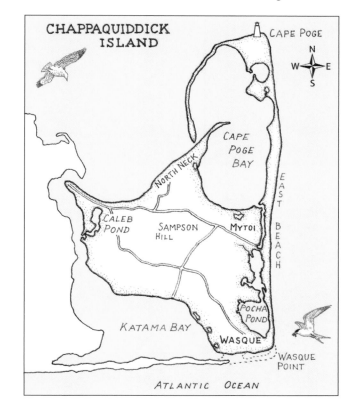

American oystercatcher and chick

easterly migration of the opening. As the breach moves east and approaches Wasque Point, the cliffs are subject to severe erosion. The beach continues to extend to the east and eventually wraps around the point, protecting the cliffs from further erosion and closing off Katama Bay until the next episode. Openings in other locations were documented in 1775, 1795, 1830, 1846, 1953, 1976, and 1991, and an opening in 1921 was the only successful one that was the result of human labor.

The most recent breach occurred in April 2007. Dramatic, though not unexpected, changes occurred at Wasque. Swan Pond disappeared, and more than 20 feet of beach at Wasque Point was washed away. A private home located at the tip of Wasque Point had to be moved back 275 feet to keep it from falling into the ocean.

Most of Wasque Reservation is flat, grassy heath-shrub community, edged by low sand cliffs and beach. Succession is under way and obvious in the uplands. Pitch pines are creeping into these upland moors, and oak woodlands can also be found. All varieties of trees have become more prominent after sheep grazing ceased. Without control by fire, mowing, or grazing, the woodland succession will continue, and the moorlike quality of Wasque will disappear. Prescribed fire undertaken by trained staff is a tool that has been used successfully to maintain grasslands here.

Wasque is a popular spot to surfcast for fish. At high tide, surfcasters and their buggies line the beach, hoping to catch striped bass, bluefish, or false albacore. Seals can sometimes be seen offshore, angling for the same delicious species.

Shorebirds, including piping plovers, terns, oystercatchers, and black skimmers, nest on the barrier beaches surrounding Wasque. Help these threatened shorebirds survive by observing posted signs and respecting seasonal closures. Don't let the fate of the heath hen befall these avian beachgoers.

TRAIL GUIDE

Due to the changing face of Wasque and the dramatic loss of land during breaches, the trail system is not static. Three parking lots offer starting points for property exploration. To follow this trail guide, begin at the parking lot at the entrance gatehouse for a comprehensive view of all the property has to offer.

Enter the property and proceed to the gatehouse. Park your vehicle in the lot adjacent to the gatehouse. **Cross the maintenance road to the north of the parking lot to find the beginning of the trailhead.** Pitch pine, *Pinus rigida*, woods beckon,

softening the trail with their fallen needles nested among the trailing arbutus, *Epigaea repens*, and pincushion moss, *Leucobryum glaucum*. The needles of pitch pine are in groups of three—think pitchfork with three tines—unlike white pine, which has needle groups of five. These utilitarian trees provided pitch and lumber for shipbuilding, their high resin content acting as a preservative to prevent decay.

Follow the trail until it meets up with the connector trail to the Martha's Vineyard Land Bank's Pocha Pond Reservation. On another trip, explore Pocha Pond Reservation and the extensive trail system that crosses Chappaquiddick. For now, **bear right** to continue on Wasque Reservation, noting the transition to oak woodlands.

A four-way intersection seems to offer options; however, the right trail takes you to the maintenance area and the left to the Pocha Pond shoreline. If you wish, **go left** to gaze across the pond, but return to **follow the original trail through the intersection** to continue on your way, keeping the pond on your left.

The oak woodlands open up to a field. **Follow the trail to the right** and meet up with the dirt road. The gatehouse where you parked is up the road to the right. **Take a left** and walk along the road toward the fishing parking lot and the water's edge. A trail will appear on your right before you reach the parking lot, which parallels the ocean. It is worth a short walk to the fishing parking lot to see spectacular ocean views, but return to the trail to stroll between the field and the ocean.

This portion of the trail allows for a true appreciation of Wasque's moors and its associated plants. Beach heather (*Hudsonia tomentosa*), lowbush blueberry (*Vaccinium angustifolium*), bearberry (*Arctostaphylos uva-ursi*), and many others provide botanical interest.

Emerge at Wasque beach and spend some time beachcombing. Edo Potter, who has been going to Chappy ever since she was a small child and now resides on Pimpneymouse Farm on Chappaquiddick, tells about picnics at Wasque when she was young. The family traveled from their farm in a horse-drawn wagon.

Shark eye

Atlantic oyster drill

Sanderlings

Edo used to chide her father because the hitching post for the horse was so far from the beach and they had such a long walk to get to the picnic spot. She saw that post go into the waves many years ago, which indicates the amount of erosion that has occurred in less than a generation's time. Edo Potter's book, *The Last Farm on Chappaquiddick* (Vineyard Stories, 2010), provides special insight on growing up on Chappaquiddick Island.

The beach at Wasque is one of the last resting places on the Vineyard for sand that has migrated from Up-Island beaches. From Wasque, some of the sand may wash around the point and along East Beach to Cape Poge, but much of it will move offshore, perhaps to become part of Skiff's Island for a while. Skiff's Island comes and goes, so it may or may not be seen on a visit.

During the winter, sea ducks fish the rip currents off the beach. Eiders and scoters are seen often. Fall brings many migrating shorebirds to rest and feed. In

Jingle shells   Oyster   Morton's egg cockle   False angel wing

summer the "peeps," small sandpipers, scurry along the beaches, particularly the inner shores. These shorebirds are a confusing lot to identify. You'll need a bird field guide to sort them out.

Among the shells you might come across are as follows:

Atlantic boat or slipper, *Crepidula fornicata*

Shark's eye, *Polinices duplicatus*

Atlantic oyster drill, *Urosalpinx cinerea*

Channeled whelk, *Busycon canaliculatus*

Knobbed whelk, *Busycon carica*

Transverse ark, *Anadara transversa*

Atlantic bay scallop, *Argopecten irradians*

Common jingle, *Anomia simplex*

Eastern oyster, *Crassostrea virginica*

Morton's egg cockle, *Laevicardium mortoni*

Chestnut astarte, *Astarte castanea*

False angel wing, *Petricola pholadiformis*

Atlantic surf clam, *Spisula solidissimia*

Where the common Northern moon shell, *Lunatia heros*, is found, look also for the uncommon shark's eye, *Polinices duplicatus*. The latter is similar, but the spire is flatter and readily identified by the large brown or purple lobe or callus that nearly covers the umbilical hole. Other rare shells that have periodically been found at Wasque include the Atlantic plate limpet, *Acmaea testudinalis*; Purplish tagelus, *Tagelus divisus*; and the Atlantic nut clam, *Nucula proxima*. A real surprise was the discovery of a sea urchin, not truly a shell, but a test, or external skeleton, from an animal that is a close relative of the sand dollar and more often inhabits warmer climes.

Leave the beach and follow the dirt road back to the gatehouse where you parked your car. This separate island, a land that time and development have only lightly touched, is one not to miss.

— **End of Trail** —

The Island's only true "tourist attraction."

Gay Head (Aquinnah)

—— FAST FACTS ——

GAY HEAD (AQUINNAH) CLIFFS AND AQUINNAH CULTURAL CENTER (EDWIN DEVRIES VANDERHOOP HOMESTEAD)

MAILING ADDRESS: Wampanoag Tribe of Gay Head (Aquinnah), 20 Black Brook Road, Aquinnah, MA 02535-1546
SITE ADDRESS: Aquinnah Circle, Aquinnah, MA • **CONTACT:** 508.645.9265; Cultural Center: 508.645.7900; fax: 508.645.3790;
hours vary seasonally. Tribal headquarters: Monday through Friday, 9 am to 5 pm; Cultural Center open seasonally
OWNERSHIP: Wampanoag Tribe of Gay Head (Aquinnah) • **FEES:** Suggested donation for adults and children
www.wampanoagtribe.net

GAY HEAD LIGHTHOUSE

MAILING ADDRESS: Owned by the Town of Aquinnah, 65 State Road, Aquinnah, MA 02535, and managed by the Martha's
Vineyard Museum, 59 School Street, Box 1310, Edgartown, MA 02539 • **SITE ADDRESS:** 9 Aquinnah Circle, Aquinnah, MA
CONTACT: 508.627.4441. Lighthouse is staffed and open to the public seasonally. Check website for hours.
OWNERSHIP: Town of Aquinnah • **FEES:** Admission fee for adults. Museum members and children under 12 are free.
www.mvmuseum.org

AQUINNAH HEADLANDS PRESERVE (NORTH AND SOUTH HEADS)

MAILING ADDRESS: Martha's Vineyard Land Bank Commission, PO Box 2057, Edgartown, MA 02539 • **SITE ADDRESS:**
Off the Aquinnah Circle, Aquinnah, MA • **CONTACT:** 508.627.7141; fax 508.627.7415; Monday through Friday, 8 am
to 4 pm • **OWNERSHIP:** Martha's Vineyard Land Bank Commission • **FEES:** Free to all • **NUMBER OF ACRES:** 49.4
www.mvlandbank.com

No island visit is complete without a trip to Gay Head /Aquinnah. Steeped in history and culture, these lands whisper secrets of geology, legend, and tragedy.

Amenities: Seasonal restrooms (fee required), limited public parking at Cliffs, town parking lot fee seasonally. For the Aquinnah Headlands Preserve: Trails on the North Head of the Aquinnah Headlands are open from September 15 to June 14; South Head trails are open year-round. Dog walking on South Head permitted from October 1 to March 30 in uplands (town bylaw prohibits dogs on the beach at all times), but no dogs on the North Head. Aquinnah Cultural Center open seasonally.

Directions to Gay Head Cliffs: Follow signs to Gay Head / Aquinnah. The road ends (State Road) at the Aquinnah Circle. Limited free parking at the top of the cliffs; municipal lot (seasonal fee) on the lower circle. Ride the Vineyard Transit Authority bus to the State Road loop. Bicycle racks are available at several locations. Walk up the stairs and between the shops and restaurants to the top of the cliff. Access the North Head of the Aquinnah Headlands via Pilot's Landing Road (no parking, on foot only) and the South Head via a trail on the lower town parking lot or at a trail at the Aquinnah Cultural Center.

Gay Head / Aquinnah

Wampanoags called this place Aquinnah, which means the "land under the hill." In 1602 explorer Bartholomew Gosnold saw this spectacular rising landform from the

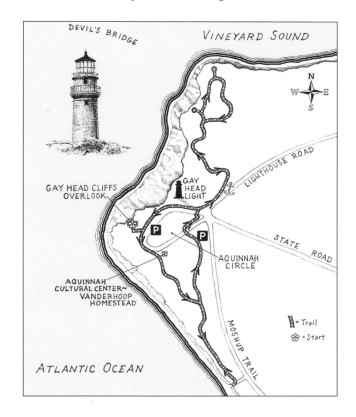

Aerial view Gay Head Cliffs

sea and called it Dover Cliffs, after the famous formation on the English Channel. Whaling ship sailors first used the name "Gay Head" to describe the "gaily colored cliffs" sometime between 1602 and 1662. In 1998 the town voted to change the name back to the original Wampanoag name, Aquinnah. Though officially Aquinnah, both names are regularly used to describe the westernmost Island town.

The cliffs at Gay Head are the Island's premier sightseeing attraction. At one time, during the Wisconsin glaciation, the high land right here stood as an island in a sea of ice with the glacier sweeping around it on all sides. Rising more than 100 feet above sea level, the Gay Head Cliffs, with their beauty and historical significance, are a designated National Natural Landmark.

The Wampanoag Tribe of Gay Head (Aquinnah) own and manage the land at the cliffs. These lands are sacred and important to tribal members culturally, historically, and economically, since all businesses at the cliffs are tribal-owned.

HISTORY Much has been written about Gay Head and the Wampanoag, the original inhabitants of Martha's Vineyard. The Wampanoag tribal community here remains strong. Their history and legends invite exploration. Visit the Aquinnah Cultural Center at the cliffs

> 66 Of all the heavenly phenomena that I have had the good fortune to witness— borealis lights, mock suns, or meteoric showers—I have never seen anything that, in mystic splendor, equaled the trick of the magic lantern of Gay Head. 99
>
> —David Hunter, Union general in the American Civil War

Gay Head light

or the Martha's Vineyard Museum, where exhibits and information about the Wampanoag can be found.

The Island's Native Americans historically belonged to one of four Wampanoag tribal areas: Takemmies lived in Tisbury; the Nunne-pogs, in Edgartown; the Aquinnahs, in Gay Head; and the Chappaquiddicks,

Vineyard painter Stan Murphy's mural of the Wampanoag creation legend

on the sometimes separate island that still bears their name. Mainland Wampanoag referred to all these groups as the Capawacks: "the people who live in the refuge place."

The Wampanoag maintain oral traditions, though others have written down their legends. Island artist Stan Murphy painted a mural in the Katharine Cornell Theatre in Vineyard Haven that depicts the Island's Wampanoag creation legend. Moshup, a mythical giant who was the first Wampanoag sachem or chief, is seen standing in the waters off the Gay Head Cliffs, holding a whale by the tail and offering it to the people of his tribe. Along the cliffs to the south is the site of Moshup's home, now known as Devil's Den, which has been used over the years for ceremonial purposes.

Moshup was known to be a "benevolent being" who wished to live in peace with all others. One of the Wampanoag myths relates that some of his people came to him asking that a bridge be built to the mainland so that visits with relatives and trading could be undertaken more readily. This also appealed to the younger generation who were restless for more social contact.

There were, of course, arguments against such a bridge. Some feared that the Island would be inundated with visitors from across the water and that in time they might come to rule the Island. The controversy became so heated that Moshup considered the situation at length before deciding what must be done.

While he was pondering, a very old woman came and asked to be heard. She suggested that he agree to build the bridge during one night when the moon was full, which he could easily do. But he could only work from sunset until the cock crowed.

So he announced that he would build a bridge of stone, under these terms, from Aquinnah to Cuttyhunk Island. From there his people could easily walk up the Elizabeth Islands to the mainland.

As the sun set on the night of the next full moon, Moshup began collecting many rocks along the shore, carrying them in his big leather apron, and then started to toss them into the water off the cliff in the direction of Cuttyhunk. He was making splendid progress when suddenly he dropped a great boulder with a yelp. One big foot came out of the water with a crab attached to a toe. With a big kick, the crab flew off and landed to the southwest, to become an island later called Noman's Land.

Moshup then came ashore to see what damage had been done and to massage the sore toe. While he was sitting on the beach, the tribe heard a cock crow and turned to see the old woman standing with her pet rooster. She had placed a light before its eyes; thinking dawn had arrived, the cock began to crow, thus signaling the end of the bridge-building episode.

The unfinished bridge is now called Devil's Bridge and is known as a notorious and dangerous spot that boats should avoid carefully. Many shipwrecks have occurred here, including the most disastrous one of the 19th century, the wreck of the *City of Columbus*. To this day, no one really knows what happened or can explain why in the early morning of January 18, 1884, only twelve hours out of Boston on her way to Savannah, the vessel went aground on Devil's Bridge.

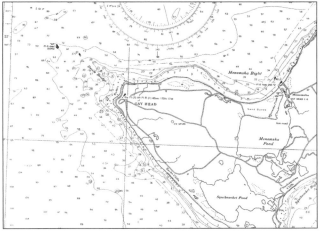

Chart of Devil's Bridge

There were 87 passengers aboard and a crew of 45. Of these, only 29 survived, all of them men, including 17 crew members and Captain S. E. Wright himself. There was a prolonged and detailed investigation, but the reason for the wreck was never fully determined and many questions remain unanswered.

The night was clear with a full moon, although a stiff northwest wind was blowing. Why was the ship so far off course? And why did the captain leave the bridge before the ship was safely out of Vineyard Sound? Why were no women or children among those saved?

The people of Gay Head had seen many wrecks before, but this was the worst. They rallied all their resources and performed many acts of great courage. Brave crews operated lifeboats. Working their way through the wreckage-strewn waters and freezing winds, they were able to rescue some men from the water and others still clinging to the rigging of the sunken vessel. Dorothy R. Scoville tells this and other dramatic stories in her book *Shipwrecks on Martha's Vineyard* (self-published, 1977).

Captain Wright was brought to trial and lost his license. He never went back to sea.

Settlement remained sparse at the cliffs. Edwin DeVries Vanderhoop, a whaling captain and the only Aquinnah Wampanoag to serve in the Massachusetts State Legislature, built a home at the cliffs in the 1890s. The Vanderhoop Homestead still remains and is now the Aquinnah Cultural Center. Its mission is to "preserve, interpret, and document the Aquinnah Wampanoag self-defined history, culture, and contributions past, present, and future."

The South Head of the Martha's Vineyard Land Bank Commission's Aquinnah Headlands Preserve was opened to the public in 1991. This property is owned and managed by the Martha's Vineyard Land Bank Commission, which was created by Island voters in 1986 in response to a booming cycle of development and associated loss of open space. After more than 25 years, over 3,000 acres have been conserved by the Land Bank. The commission's revenue is generated by a 2 percent public surcharge on most real estate transfers occurring in the six towns of Martha's Vineyard. The Aquinnah Headlands North Head property was opened in 2011.

NATURAL FEATURES The cliffs themselves are a geologist's history book. Deposits from three separate geologic time periods are exposed at this site in crumpled disarray, the product of glacial disturbance.

The oldest are the 100-million-year-old Cretaceous deposits, which lie at the bottom of the cliff and are often hidden. The Miocene greensands and other preglacial deposits date from 30 million years to 2 million years ago at the beginning of the Pleistocene glaciation. The late Clifford Kaye of the U.S. Geological Service, who spent many years studying the geology of the Vineyard, described this as the richest exposure of the Pleistocene period in the world. All geologists may not agree, but even a layperson will find the cliffs dramatic today, despite the fact that the spectacular red clay is slowly disappearing as the result of natural and human-induced forces.

Because of the erosion of the cliffs, regulations (and common sense) now prohibit climbing on them and removing clay from the site. Erosion occurs from both the sea's action and as a result of the seepage from the water table behind (landward) the cliffs. The seepage creates slick surfaces that allow sections of the cliffs to slip and slide downward and finally crash upon the beach. Most of the material that the sea sweeps away comes from these slides.

Much as one may regret the erosion of the cliffs, the process will eventually expose similar deposits that underlie much of the Island. Thick streaks of clay are often visible during construction Up-Island.

We can thank the glaciers for the beauty of the cliffs today. The power and energy behind the ice in the Pleistocene glaciers disrupted the Vineyard's underground deposits, forcing them upward into great folds and faults, much like the curved compression of ribbon candy. Subsequent erosion over thousands of years has revealed the profusion of color and texture that still lies buried from sight elsewhere. Before the glaciers distorted them, the deposits were in relatively flat layers, each representing a specific period of time, sometimes hundreds of thousands or millions of years, when climatic conditions and the sea level remained relatively stable. There are some gaps in the history, such as the Tertiary period during which erosion erased some sediments. Although the history is incomplete

Gay Head Cliffs

and interpretations may vary, the sequence of events is becoming clearer and more detailed. For more information about the deposits in the cliffs, see the chapter in this book titled, "The Hidden History of Martha's Vineyard."

TRAIL GUIDE

Start by walking up to the overlook at the Gay Head Cliffs. On a day with good visibility, you can see the coastline of the mainland in the far background and, nearer, the chain of the Elizabeth Islands. From left to right, Cuttyhunk, the governmental center of the chain, is the first island. The island of Penikese lies north of it, just out of sight. The Canapitsit Channel, invisible from this vantage point, separates Cuttyhunk from Nashawena Island. The next hole, as these passageways are named, is Quicks Hole, and through it, New Bedford can be seen on the mainland. The next island is Pasque. Between it and Naushon lies Robinsons Hole. Beyond, with good visibility, you can see Falmouth on the coast of Cape Cod, separated from Naushon by Woods Hole.

Turn around and look to the south to find the island of Noman's Land located three miles off the Vineyard coast. Noman's Land was likely named after the Wampanoag sachem Tequenoman, who ruled this area when settlers came. This 628-acre island was used as a bombing range by the U.S. Navy from 1942 to 1996. The U.S. Fish and Wildlife Service now owns the island, and it is a wildlife refuge primarily for migratory birds. The island is off-limits to visitors, closed for safety and for wildlife protection.

Enjoy the views, and when you are ready to continue your Gay Head exploration, **return to the Aquinnah Circle. Turn right and follow the road** around the circle counterclockwise. A solitary home beckons: the Vanderhoop Homestead, now the Aquinnah Cultural Center. If it is open, explore the museum and perhaps take a house tour to learn more about Wampanoag history and culture.

At the southwest corner of the Aquinnah Cultural Center, find the Martha's Vineyard Land Bank trailhead to take you to Moshup Beach. Following signs to the beach, the trail continues on land owned by the Sheriff's Meadow Foundation and the Town of Aquinnah and merges with the trail from the town parking lot.

This trail takes you through coastal shrublands and grasslands that contain both native and nonnative species. Look for the natives: blue flag irises that bloom in late spring, poison ivy, prickly dewberry, fescue grass,

Vanderhoop Homestead

cow parsnip, arrowwood, and bayberry. Beach rose *(Rosa rugosa)*, bittersweet, Russian olive, and Japanese black pine are the botanical washashores, nonnative species brought by people, birds, or the sea.

Watch your step on the eroded path, and emerge on Moshup Beach. This scenic beach offers peace and beauty in the off-season. However, when summer comes, the beach is incredibly popular, with beachgoers sometimes sharing space with the piping plovers that can nest here.

Notice the freshwater streams that drain directly into the ocean. Spend some time walking along the shoreline to the north to appreciate the cliffs from below.

Remember to respect the prohibition on taking clay or climbing the cliffs.

When you are ready to leave the beach, return to the trail that you walked down, **only take the right fork** when you have an option. This trail leads you to the lower parking area and the lower end of Aquinnah Circle. **Check the map station** to help you find your way to the North Head of Aquinnah Headlands Preserve.

Cross through the town parking lot and continue on Aquinnah Circle counterclockwise. Take Lighthouse Road and walk along the road's edge until you come to the first driveway. A large white anchor can be seen. Access

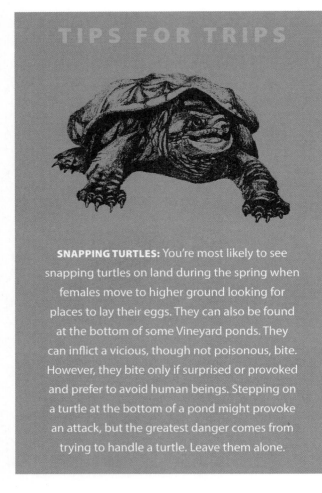

TIPS FOR TRIPS

SNAPPING TURTLES: You're most likely to see snapping turtles on land during the spring when females move to higher ground looking for places to lay their eggs. They can also be found at the bottom of some Vineyard ponds. They can inflict a vicious, though not poisonous, bite. However, they bite only if surprised or provoked and prefer to avoid human beings. Stepping on a turtle at the bottom of a pond might provoke an attack, but the greatest danger comes from trying to handle a turtle. Leave them alone.

the North Head Trails (open September 15 to June 14 only) by skirting along this driveway to the left to find the beginning of the trail. Land Bank signs farther up the trail will confirm that you are on the correct trail. Please be respectful of the nearby private properties.

The North Head Trail loops through shrublands and grasslands. Two overlooks off of the main loop trail provide stunning views. Follow the Land Bank signs to the first overlook, **staying on the left** when the trail forks. **Reach the southern lookout by taking another left.**

In the winter, look for large rafts of sea ducks. Both the North and South Heads are important for migrating birds and butterflies. Hawks, waterfowl, and warblers can be seen passing here during their fall and spring migrations. Birds flying over land are concentrated in this area because the combination of land and wind creates a funnel effect. Birds are pushed by the prevailing winds to the coast and follow the coastline before heading out to sea. The perched wetlands and shrublands provide the cover and habitat they need.

This area was known as Steamboat Landing. A pier first permitted in 1883 allowed for sightseeing excursion by passengers on the Martha's Vineyard, New Bedford, and Nantucket Steamship Company boats. In

1885, following the *City of Columbus* shipwreck tragedy, a U.S. lifesaving station was built and put into operation.

From the overlook, go back to the Loop Trail and take a left to continue. A second, more northern lookout **(trail on the left)** provides a bench to take a moment and take in the ocean view.

Erosion is changing the face of this cliff and the lands behind it. Estimates of the loss of land are two to four feet per year; with a powerful storm, however, it would be possible to lose 50 feet in an hour. Records indicate that since 1951, more than 90 feet have been lost. At that rate, the North Head could be lost in less than 200 years.

Similar to the plants at the South Head, sumac, thistle, viburnum, oak, and daisy are just a few of the plants encountered in the shrubland and grassland community along the loop trail. Yellow thistle begs a second look; notice that it is not the more commonly seen purple thistle.

Complete the loop and head back to Lighthouse Road and onto Aquinnah Circle. The final stop is the Gay Head Lighthouse on the right side of the circle. This iconic lighthouse is the only Island lighthouse made of brick. It was requested in 1796 to assist ships passing through the treacherous Devil's Bridge area. The lighthouse went into service in 1799.

Thistle

The lighthouse's first keeper was Ebenezer Skiff, who also had the distinction of being the first non-Wampanoag to live in Gay Head. He was paid just $200 per year to operate and secure this remote Island lighthouse. Its first light was a spider lamp, which was replaced by a parabolic lens. In 1855 a Fresnel lens with more than 1,000 prisms was installed. This lens would eventually be replaced with a modern aero beacon. The Gay Head Lighthouse Fresnel lens can still be seen on the Edgartown campus of the Martha's Vineyard Museum. The historical light had a flash of three whites and one red; however, this signal was changed to its current single red-and-white flash at 15-second intervals.

The lighthouse was built and operated by the U.S. government, but it was declared surplus in 2012. The Town of Aquinnah voted to take ownership of this historic structure. Having been moved back from the cliff's edge once, in 1844, erosion again threatens the tower. Another move is imminent as erosion averages two feet per year, and only 50 feet remain from the lighthouse to the cliff. Due to this vulnerability, the National Trust of Historic Places put the Aquinnah Lighthouse on its 2013 list of America's most endangered historic places.

Take a tour to learn more about this historic structure if the lighthouse is open.

"Go west" is great advice to Islanders or visitors alike. Truly, no trip to the Island is complete without a journey to this remote westerly wonderland.

— **End of Trail** —

CHAPTER FOUR

Beetlebung
A Guide to Island Flora

Live in each season as it passes; breathe the air, drink the drink,
taste the fruit, and resign yourself to the influence of the earth.

—Henry David Thoreau

slanders have their own special language. The titles of this and the next chapter—"Beetlebung" and "Pinkletink"—call attention to unique local names that identify a tree and a frog, respectively. Together, they represent the members of the plant and animal kingdoms found on the Island. The beetlebung tree elsewhere is known as the tupelo or black/sour gum, *Nyssa sylvatica*. "Pinkletink" is the term used on the Island for the frog known as spring peeper in other parts of its range and recognized worldwide as *Pseudacris crucifer*.

With its moderate climate, the Island belies the fact that it is situated in cold New England. Its weather more strongly resembles the mid-Atlantic region than Massachusetts. The Island receives less snow and maintains milder temperatures than that of the mainland, and its plants reflect those conditions.

As an island, our flora is isolated and is highly affected by the forces of wind, salt, and water. While we have a smaller diversity of plants, we have a high occurrence of rarities.

Perhaps the greatest threat to the Island's flora is the appearance and success of many invasive species. Oriental bittersweet, common reed (Phragmites), autumn olive, codium (dead man's fingers) seaweed, and many others threaten to overwhelm our native plants. Planting, cultivating, and protecting native species is vital to preserving the island's unique floral heritage.

To get to know this botanical bounty, the list below describes the plants that are likely to be seen on the Island. Learning the basics of plant parts and using the keys will help you begin to be able to identify and enjoy most of the island's flora.

SEAWEEDS AND OTHER MARINE ALGAE Seaweeds are simple and primitive plants and vary considerably in appearance. Although some have complex structures and forms, none have true roots, stems, or leaves. Seaweeds have holdfasts that look like roots, stipes that are stemlike, and a leaflike part called a blade. They absorb carbon dioxide, water, and nutrients through all these parts. In general, seaweeds are grouped and identified by color.

Fire Algae—Pyrrophyta

The fire algae include the dinoflagellates and are sometimes classified as plants and sometimes as animals because different species possess characteristics of each. Some species of the microscopic dinoflagellates can cause red tides, or as scientists prefer to call them, harmful algal blooms (HABs). When these algae grow excessively, or bloom, the water can become discolored. Different varieties are capable of causing irritation to the eyes and respiratory system, bioluminescence, and the poisoning of shellfish and those who eat them.

Green Seaweeds—Chlorophyta

Green seaweeds contain chlorophyll and are found in shallower water than the others.

Sea grass, mermaid or maiden hair, *Enteromorpha* spp. These plants appear as long tubes, singly or in colonies. Their basal disc attaches to stone and wood in the intertidal zone. An interesting characteristic of this seaweed is its tolerance to wide changes in salinity.

Sea lettuce, *Ulva lactuca*, is lettucelike, thin, almost translucent bright, light green, and found in shallow water. In its folds you can find many small marine animals. Although it has a holdfast, it is often found free-floating in masses on the bottoms of shallow pools and brackish ponds. Sea lettuce is edible, although care should be taken if harvesting for consumption since it can also survive in polluted waters.

Oyster thief, sputnik weed, sea stag horn, dead man's finger, or spaghetti grass, *Codium fragile*, is a nonnative seaweed that hails from the Pacific. It was first reported on Long Island in 1957. It is an erect, bifurcated (branches in twos), dark green plant that is quite buoyant. When alive it resembles a green sponge and attaches itself by holdfast to shells and rocks. In its reproductive stage it accumulates oxygen and floats away with whatever it is attached to (often shellfish)—hence the name, "oyster thief."

Brown Algae—Phaeophyta

Brown algae also contain chlorophyll, but it is masked by other chemicals. Most of these plants turn black when dried.

Kelp, *Laminaria* spp., has a long, leaflike blade and a holdfast that attaches to rocks, wharfs, and jetties. Several other similar plants, including **sea lace**, *Chorda filum*, can sometimes wash ashore after storms and are found most often along South Beach.

Rockweed or sea wrack, *Fucus* spp., grows near the high-water mark, so is often exposed by the receding tide. More olive-green than brown, its flat and leathery fronds are paired with oval air sacs and forked branching, usually in twos. Sea wrack grows by holdfast to stones, rocks, and wharf pilings. Bladders of these species, and almost all the rockweeds, make a popping sound when pinched.

Knotted wrack or **rockweed**, *Ascophyllum nodosum*, is found in intertidal areas of lagoons and other sheltered saltwater areas, and is the same color as rockweed. It is a more slender plant, with bladders on its stem, and stalks branching from the main stem.

Sargassum, *Sargassum filipendula*, has air bladders growing from the attachments on the leaflike lobes and serrated blades. It is a common benthic (bottom-dwelling) species.

Red Algae—Rhodophyta

These seaweeds are more highly developed than others. Many are used for food. They tend to grow in deeper water than the wracks and rockweeds and need to be covered by water most of the time.

Laver, red and purple, *Porphyra leucosticta* and *P. umbilicalis*, are lookalikes similar to sea lettuce except for color. Members of the Porphyra genus are known more commonly as *nori*, the popular seaweed used in sushi here and in Asia.

Irish moss, *Chondrus crispus*, is found just below the normal low-tide mark. Deep purple or purple-green and almost iridescent when fresh, it grows in dense clumps. It is usually seen in the wrack line on outer beaches. A gel-forming extract from Irish moss, carrageenan, is used in the preparation of many foods (including ice cream), pharmaceutical and cosmetic products, and in a variety of other processes, including clarifying beer and meat packing.

Common coralline, *Corallina officinalis*, lives below the zone of Irish moss. It is an erect plant growing from a basal disc. Common coralline can extract lime from the sea and incorporate it into its tissues and along the stems, but not at joints. There are several species. Pinkish-white in color, some form flat patches on rocks while others are bushy in form. This seaweed turns white when dry and is found from Long Island to Newfoundland throughout the year.

Dulse, *Palmeria palmata*, fronds are nearly two feet long with an inconspicuous stalk rising from a small, disclike holdfast. Its leathery purple or red blades up to six inches wide split into two or more divisions. It is edible and can be chewed like gum.

Chenille weed, *Dasya* spp., has a slender stem rising from a small disc-shaped holdfast and branches freely. Feathery fronds are clothed with small hairs, reddish pink to deep wine in color, that adhere well to paper and make an attractive decoration.

Grinnellia americana is a strikingly beautiful, thin, rosy-pink blade with ruffled edges. It appears quite suddenly in midsummer and disappears as quickly several weeks later.

REFERENCES

Andrew, Jennifer, and Inga Fredland. *A Field Guide to the Marine Life of Nantucket* (Maria Mitchell Association, 2001). A useable guide to the marine life of the Cape and Islands.

Hillson, C. J. *Seaweeds* (Pennsylvania State University Press, 1977). Lists, illustrates and describes over eighty species.

Kingsbury, John M. *Seaweeds of Cape Cod and the Islands* (Chatham Press, 1969). Local book, can likely be found in Island libraries.

Treat, Rose. *The Seaweed Book: How to Find and Have Fun with Seaweed* (Star Bright Books, 1995). An introduction to the seaweeds found around the Vineyard.

Villalard-Bohnsack, Martine. *Illustrated Key to the Seaweeds of New England* (Rhode Island Natural History Survey, 2003).

LICHENS You may not know what a lichen is, although you probably have noticed them on the bark of trees or even trod upon them as you walked the Island's trails or open fields. Lichen usually go unrecognized as plants at all. It has been estimated that there are probably at least 100 different species on the Island.

Lichens are a primitive organism. Scientists have found evidence of them going back through three-quarters of the earth's life, long before the higher plants evolved. They play an important role as pioneers in soil production. The acids they produce decompose rocks and dead plants and add humus to the soil as they decay. Lichens are indicators of unpolluted air. You will be unlikely to find lichens in a city, but if you do, feel comfortable about the quality of the air you are breathing.

Actually, lichens are two interdependent organisms, a fungus and an alga. The role of each is not entirely clear, but apparently the fungus supports the plant and retains moisture. The alga photosynthesizes and produces food for the plant. If you find yourself walking on a patch of crunchy, gray, mosslike plants, pick up a piece. You are looking at lichen. If you save some and later set it in a little water, you'll see that it absorbs an enormous quantity in a short time. They can endure long periods of drought, even years, and an incredible range of temperatures. Some endure the heat of sun-baked rocks; others flourish in the coldest spots on earth. Their ecological range accounts for their inclusion among the pioneer plants.

Lichens are of little use as food for wildlife on the Vineyard, although in the tundra, reindeer and other browsers eat reindeer moss, which is not a true moss but lichen. Some birds—such as the hummingbird, wood pewee, and blue-gray gnatcatcher—use fragments of lichens to line their nests. Some lichens are used to manufacture antibiotics, and for a long time lichens have been employed as dye for Harris tweeds.

Lichens are common on the Island, growing on rocks, trees, sand, and bare or impoverished ground. Three different forms can be easily found: crustose (crusty), foliose (leaflike), and fruiticose (shrubby) with many intergrades. A few easily identified common ones are listed below.

Cladoniaceae

Reindeer moss, *Cladonia* spp. Several species are found in large patches on soil in sandy areas where they are protected from salt air by dunes or vegetation.

   British soldiers, *Cladonia cristatella*, and **pixie cups**, *Cladonia pyxidata*, are often found growing amid the reindeer moss. Look first for the bright red fruiting tops of the British soldiers, and almost assuredly you will also find the tiny goblet-shaped pixie cups.

Usneae

Old man's beard, *Usneae barbata*. A fruiticose, grayish, yellow-green lichen often seen hanging from dead branches of beach plum and other trees and bushes.

   Yellow wall lichen, *Xanthoria parietina*. A foliose lichen that grows on rocks and shingles near salt water. It also prefers some lime, as in cement mortar.

FUNGI

You probably recognize a mushroom when you see it. What you see is only the fruiting body of the mushroom. The rest of the organism, the vegetative matter known as mycelium, lives in the ground or within decaying plant material.

   Examine the underside of a mushroom and you will see gill-like structures or pores. Some are funnel-shaped, others look like corals, and still others are puffballs. Some, indluding bracket fungi, grow as shelf-like structures on tree trunks.

   In order to become familiar with the different species, you need to spend a good deal of time in the field studying them. There are many, and some are easily confused with others.

   Never eat any mushroom unless you are absolutely sure of its safety. From Lindsey Lee's *Edible Wild Plants of Martha's Vineyard* comes this herbalist's advice regarding mushrooms: "To conclude, few of them are good to be eaten, and most do suffocate and strangle the eater. Therefore I give my advice unto those that do love such strange and newfangled meates, to beware of licking honey among thorns, least the sweetness of the one that do not countervail the sharpness and pricking of the other."

   The **Amanitaceae** family includes the **fly amanita**, *Amanita muscaria*, and **destroying angel**, *Amanita verna*. They are among the most poisonous of mushrooms.

Earth stars, *Geaster hygrometricus*, are often associated with the Cladonia lichens. They look like a star-shaped piece of leather and if fresh will still have the puffball intact. When the plant dries, the "star" curls around the puffball until the next rain. At that time it opens again, arching off the ground and forcing the spores to fly out.

REFERENCES

Barron, George. *Mushrooms of Northeast North America* (Lone Pine Publishing, 1999).

Lincoff, Gary H. *National Audubon Society Field Guide to North American Mushrooms* (Knopf, 1981).

Miller, Orson K., Jr. *Mushrooms of North America* (Dutton, 1977).

MOSSES Mosses are small, soft plants that brighten up the woodlands in all seasons. Growing in clumps or mats, moss can be found on many surfaces, though they thrive best in moist habitats. Mosses lack flowers, seeds, and true roots, reproducing vegetatively or by spores and holding on with their rhizoids or rootlets. Their water-loving ways and supple surface encouraged their historical uses as bedding, insulation, wound dressing, and even diapers.

Sphagnum moss, *Sphagnum* spp. Identification of individual species is complicated, and no attempt is made here as they look so much alike superficially. Sphagnum moss is an indicator plant for freshwater wetlands.

Hair-cap moss, *Polytrichum* spp. Again, identification is difficult. This genus of mosses is often seen with lichens in open fields and woodland edges.

REFERENCES

Bland, John. *Forests of Lilliput: The Realm of Mosses and Lichen* (Prentice Hall, 1971).

HORSETAILS

The genus Equisetum is the sole survivor whose ancestors formed forests in the Carboniferous period. There is no known inventory for this genus on the Island, although *Equisetum arvense*, the field horsetail, has been identified (Leahy) as "rather local at Felix Neck."

CLUB-MOSSES

Genus *Lycopodium* grows on the Vineyard, but is scarce and local. Find it in cooler, dry, sandy areas in open woodlands or open pastures. Club-mosses are living descendants of primitive plants. Ground pine, *L. irislachyum*, is seen in several places Up-Island. It grows like tiny evergreen trees usually topped by a candelabra of four cones.

FERNS Ferns are also plants with primitive ancestors. Among the earliest plants to evolve, they often grew in tree form as they do today in the tropics. Other plants with deeply cut foliage might be confused with ferns. Yarrow is one. To differentiate this plant from a fern, brush the leaf in question; if it feels "feather" soft, it is the native flowering plant yarrow, *Achillea millefolium*.

To distinguish ferns from other plants in the spring, examine the tips of the leaves. If coiled they are ferns; if not, they are flowering plants. Another distinction is that ferns will not develop buds or flowers as they grow. The spring-emerging coiled fronds are known as fiddleheads. The most commonly consumed fiddleheads are the young growth of the ostrich fern, which are generally not found growing wild on the Vineyard. Although other varieties of fern fiddleheads are thought to be edible, some are believed to be carcinogenic, so care should be taken if considering harvesting fiddleheads for food.

Fern species are most easily identified by the arrangement of sori or fruit dots. Some ferns have separate fertile fronds. Fronds are the entire fern leaf, including blade and stipe. For the others, examine the underside of the fronds to find fertile ones and compare the patterns of the sori with those in a field guide.

Cinnamon fern, *Osmunda cinnamomea*, has separate fertile fronds, and they are the first to appear and first to wither. When they make their appearance they are bright green, but soon turn cinnamon-brown. The royal and interrupted ferns belong to the same genus. Cinnamon fern is the most common of the *Osmundas*.

Interrupted fern, *Osmunda claytoniana*, has two to four leaflets or pinnae in the middle of the frond that carry the sori. These wither and blacken as the sori ripen, making the fern look blighted.

Royal fern, *Osmunda regalis*, has fertile parts at the tip of the plant.

Sensitive fern or bead fern, *Onoclea sensibilis*, fronds are quite coarse-looking and have separate fertile fronds. The sori ripen into black, beadlike dots along a separate stem, hence the second name.

The somewhat similar-looking **netted chain fern**, *Woodwardia areolata*, is smaller; the fronds are a glossy green, less coarse and almost translucent. With this species, the sori are on the back of the leaves, oblong and one-third to two-fifths of an inch long in rows parallel to the midvein. As they ripen, the leaflets curl inward and can be identified at a glance by noting the difference in appearance between narrow fertile and wider infertile fronds.

Cinnamon fern

Royal fern

Interrupted fern

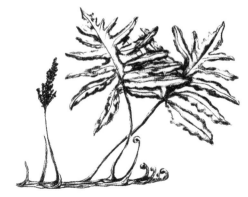

Sensitive fern

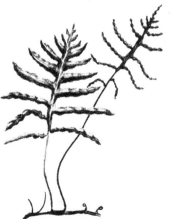

Netted chain fern

Virginia chain fern, *Woodwardia virginica*, belongs to the same genus as the netted chain fern but might be mistaken for cinnamon fern. The Virginia chain fern produces leaves singly along the rootstocks, whereas the cinnamon fern fronds grow in clumps. The sori also appear along the midvein in parallel ranks along the leaflets of the Virginia chain fern, another way to distinguish it from the cinnamon fern.

Marsh fern, *Thelypteris palustris*, is one of the common ferns of sunny, wet places. Small, delicate fronds grow singly. The sori appear in middle or late July. At that time this fern can be identified by noting fertile fronds. These are somewhat taller than the infertile fronds, and their tips appear pointed as the small, kidney-shaped sori enlarge to cover most of the back of the leaflet, causing it to roll inward.

Hay-scented or boulder fern, *Dennstaedtia punctilobula*, is another common fern of the Vineyard but is found in drier habitats. Its fronds are long, pale green and widest at the base, tapering to a slender tip. A fragrance is released when the fronds are crushed, from which the fern derives its name. The fruit dots are very small, placed at the margins of leaflets, and mature in late summer and autumn.

Bracken fern, *Pteridium aquilinum*, is a very common fern especially on dry, poor, and barren soil in full sun, and in woods, old pastures, and semi-shaded areas. The fronds are divided into three equal parts, and each is cut into leaflets and subleaflets. It is a coarse and strong plant. The narrow tips of leaflets, its variable subleaflets, and smooth, grooved stalk identify this species.

The next two ferns are often found in the richer woodlands of the western section of the moraine.

New York fern, *Thelypteris noveboracensis*, is common in sunny spots of mixed woodlands and on drier edges of swamps, in contrast to the marsh fern, which prefers a wetter habitat. The double-tapering leaf, top and bottom, is distinctive. It commonly grows in semi-tufts of three fronds.

Lady fern, *Athyrium filix-femina*, is rather large and showy with lacy-cut leaves. It is variable in shape and color. The lax, drooping tips, growth in circular clusters, and smooth stalks with few pale scales are the field characteristics. It is common in fairly moist, semi-shaded habitats.

REFERENCES

Cobb, Boughton, and Cheryl Lowe. *Peterson Field Guide to Ferns: Northeastern and Central North America* (Houghton Mifflin Harcourt, 2005). Also covers the horsetail and club mosses.

Hallowell, Anne C., and Barbara G. Hallowell. *Fern Finder* (Nature Study Guild Publishers, 2001).

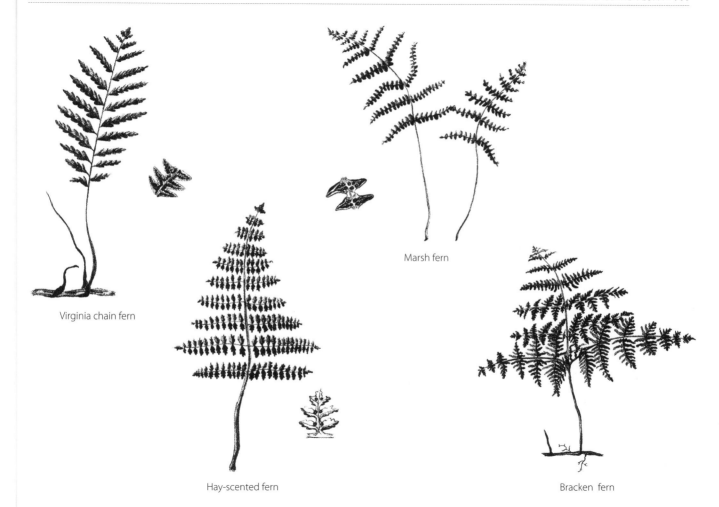

Virginia chain fern

Hay-scented fern

Marsh fern

Bracken fern

GRASSES AND GRASSLIKE PLANTS Grasses are plants in the Poaceae family and are distinguished by their narrow leaves with parallel veins and small inconspicuous flowers. Their stems are hollow and jointed, leaves sheathed, and seeds grainlike. This family is valued as an important food source since it includes wheat, barley, rye, and oats.

Beach grass, *Ammophila breviligulata*, is tall, growing to three and a half feet. Its basal leaves have sawtooth edges that often trace circles in the sand. The plant spreads by means of long underground rhizomes, and the whole plant can survive partial burying by sand. Close examination of the base of the leaves may reveal salt crystals. Beach grass can tolerate salt water by exuding the salt through its leaves. In very hot, dry weather the leaves roll up to protect the plants from dehydration. Beach grass is found on sand dunes and beaches and in sandy soils.

Little bluestem or **poverty grass**, *Schizachyrium scoparium*, is the most common grass in dry fields. This grass is conspicuous in the fall when the plants turn a blush color.

Velvet grass, *Holcus lanatus*, has gray-green, velvety leaves, the only grass in this area with such a texture.

Purple love grass, tumble-grass, or **petticoat climber**, *Eragrostis spectabilis*, is common particularly in sandy soil. The flowers are purple in late summer and early fall, and it breaks off and rolls around like a tumbleweed when ripe.

Cordgrass, *Spartina alternifolia*, is tall with coarse leaves and grows at the outer, lower edge of the salt marsh, nearest the water.

Salt meadow grass, *Spartina patens*, also known as salt marsh hay, is fine-textured and adapted to growing in the higher, upland marsh where the salt marsh is only covered by flood and storm tides.

Spike grass, *Distichlis spicata*, has leaves that stand out at an angle from the stem. Ducks eat its stems, rootstocks, and seeds. It grows at the back (landward side) of the salt marsh.

Panic grass or **switchgrass**, *Panicum virgatum*, is one of many hundreds of species in this genus. Although not evergreen, it turns yellow, adding a bright note to the gray days and dull landscapes from late fall through early spring. A common grass of the tall prairie in damp areas, on the Vineyard it grows in clumps along the upland edge of salt marshes and is often seen along roadsides.

Deer tongue, *Panicum clandestinum*, is a wide-leaved grass that grows in wetlands.

Common reed, *Phragmites australis*, is a quickly spreading, invasive plant that is a sign of disturbed land.

Common reed is often seen at the edge of salt marshes, where it tends to create a monoculture. Common reed, often called phragmites, is spreading throughout the Northeast and resists eradication. Cutting and burning only seem to encourage its growth. The big purple, feathery flowers turn gray as the fruit develops.

Eelgrass, *Zostera marina*, is not a true grass. It is a vascular plant and belongs categorized with its seed-bearing relatives.

SEDGES AND RUSHES Sedges have edges, and rushes are round. The flower clusters of sedges disintegrate when rubbed between fingers; those of rushes do not.

Chairmaker's bulrush, *Scirpus americanus* (*Schoenoplectus americanis*), grows on brackish shores.

Dark green bulrush, *Scirpus atrovirens*, flowers in late spring and disappears by summer, in wetlands.

Salt-marsh bulrush, *Scirpus robustus* (*Bolboschoenus robustus*), grows in salt and brackish water and is usually seen at the back of salt marshes.

Soft rush, *Juncus effusus*, is a common rush in fresh wetlands.

Blackgrass, *Juncus gerardii*, is a little green rush found at the back of the marsh.

Path rush, *Juncus tenuis*, grows in dry soils, usually where foot traffic is heavy.

REFERENCES

Brown, Lauren. *Grasses: An Identification Guide* (Houghton Mifflin Harcourt, 1992), is an easy-to-use guide to commonly found grasses. Includes some common sedges, rushes, and reeds.

Knobel, Edward. *Field Guide to the Grasses, Sedges, and Rushes of the United States* (Dover Publications, 1977). More comprehensive and more technical.

SEED-BEARING PLANTS
Flowering Plants (Wildflowers)

Many of the wildflowers that bloom in summer are found in open areas. The woodland flowers usually bloom in the spring before the foliage is on the trees. Shrubs bearing conspicuous flowers are included in the "Key to Woody Plants."

The list that follows includes wildflowers that bloom in the summer that are threatened by reason of their susceptibility to picking, digging, or the disturbance of their habitat. Do not pick the Island's wildflowers. Leaving them where they are growing allows others to enjoy them and ensures reproduction and their presence for years to come.

★**Arethusa,** *Arethusa bulbosa*. Bogs and wet meadows.

Birdsfoot trefoil, *Lotus corniculatus*. Fields and roadsides.

Black-eyed Susan, *Rudbeckia* spp. Dry to moist open places.

Blue vervain, *Verbena hastata*. Moist thickets, shores, and meadows.

*Bushy rockrose, *Crocanthemum dumosum*. Dry, sandy plains.

**Butterfly weed, *Asclepias tuberosa*. Dry, open fields.

Cardinal flower, *Lobelia cardinalis*. Stream banks and damp meadows.

Downy false foxglove, *Aureolaria virginica*. Edges of dry oak woods.

Fernleaf false foxglove, *Aureolaria pedicularia*. Edges of dry oak woods.

Grass pink, *Calopogon tuberosus*. Bogs and wet meadows.

Ladies' tresses, *Spiranthes* spp. Dry fields, open woods; moist meadows and swamps.

**Little ladies' tresses, *Spiranthes tuberosa*, Dry fields, open woods.

Purple gerardia, *Agalinis* spp. Moist meadows and bogs.

Rose pogonia, *Pogonia ophioglossoides*. Bogs.

*Sandplain blue-eyed grass, *Sisyrinchium fuscatem*. Sandy, open fields.

*Seabeach knotweed, *Polygonum glaucum*. Flat, sandy beach areas.

Sea lavender, also called **marsh rosemary**, *Limonium* spp. Salt marshes and beaches.

Seaside gerardia, *Agalinis maritima*. Salt marshes.

Swamp azalea, *Rhododendron viscosum*. A woody shrub that grows in swamps and wet thickets.

Swamp rose mallow, *Hibiscus moscheutos*. Brackish or fresh marshes. Also a white form, *H. palustris Peckii*, in wet meadows and pond edges.

Turk's cap lily, *Lilium superbum*. Damp meadows and edges of woods.

Wood lily, *Lilium philadelphicum*. Dry thickets and fields.

---

* Found on the Massachusetts List of Endangered, Threatened and Special Concern Species as defined in Section 10.60 of Chapter 321 of the Code of Massachusetts Regulations. The MESA List is prepared under the authority of the Massachusetts Endangered Species Act (MESA) and the Natural Heritage and Endangered Species Program (NHESP).

** Found on the Plant Watch List compiled by the NHESP. The Plant Watch List is an unofficial, nonregulatory list of plants of known or suspected conservation concern that NHESP is interested in tracking.

FOR FIELD IDENTIFICATION OF THESE AND OTHER WILDFLOWERS SEE ONE OF THE FOLLOWING GUIDES:

Hinds, Harold R., and Wilfred A. Hathaway. *Wildflowers of Cape Cod* (Chatham Press, 1968). Identifies wildflowers by habitat.

Newcomb, Lawrence. *Newcomb's Wildflower Guide* (Little, Brown and Co., 1989). The best for those who want an easy and reliable field guide. A simple key stresses the flower type (number of petals), plant type (wildflower, shrub, or vine), and characteristics of leaf type (no apparent leaves, leaves entire, leaves toothed or lobed, leaves divided).

Peterson, Roger Tory, and Margaret McKenny. *A Field Guide to Wildflowers* (Houghton Mifflin Harcourt, 1998). A visual approach; wildflowers are arranged first by color, then by form, and detail.

Stokes, Donald, and Lillian Stokes. *A Guide to Enjoying the Wildflowers* (Little, Brown & Co., 1986). Helps to understand the whole lives of selected wildflowers.

CONIFERS

Key to Red Cedar and the Pines

Red cedar and pines are conifers. Conifers can be described as cone-bearing trees and shrubs that have "naked seeds," meaning that they are not enclosed in an ovary. These plants do not produce flowers or fruit, and most are evergreens with needle or scalelike foliage.

Plants are classified according to their characteristics. By making observations, keys can be used to aid in identifying groups of plants. Dichotomous keys are organized sets of questions or characteristics that logically work through a process to identify a species. For this key to red cedar and the pines, first look closely at your evergreen. Start with Question A and choose the answer below it that most describes the plant. Follow along until a positive identification (bold name of species) is made.

QUESTION A: *What is the shape of its leaves?*

- If leaves are scalelike, it is a **Red Cedar**, *Juniperus virginiana.*
- If leaves are needlelike, in sheathed bundles, go to Question B.

QUESTION B: *How many needles are in a bundle?*

- If there are five needles in each bundle, then you have **White Pine**, *Pinus strobus.*

- If there are three needles in a bundle, it is **Pitch Pine**, *Pinus rigida*, the only native pine.
- If there are two needles in a bundle, go to Question C.

QUESTION C: *Which best matches the size and characteristics of the two needles of the bundle?*

- If they are four to six inches long and break easily, then it is a **Red Pine**, *Pinus resinosa*.
- If they are three to six inches long, stiff, and do not break when bent, then it is an **Austrian Pine**, *Casuarina equisetifolia*.
- If they are three to four inches long, stiff, and prickly when the tuft end is touched, then it is a **Japanese black pine**, *Pinus thunbergiana*.
- If they are two to three inches long, blue-green, and twisted, then it is a **Scotch pine**, *Pinus sylvestris*.
- If the needles of the bundles are very short, then it is a **Jack** or **scrub pine**, *Pinus banksiana*.

SHRUBS AND TREES Deciduous trees have broad leaves, not needles or scales that are shed in winter. **American holly**, *Ilex opaca*, is a native broadleaf tree that is not deciduous. Its leaves are thick, usually shiny, and have fierce prickles along the edges.

The key below will help you identify common shrubs and trees by their characteristics. These characteristics include plant type (tree, shrub, or vine), leaf and branch arrangement (opposite, whorled, or alternate), and leaf type (toothed, lobed, divided, or compound). From each category, choose the number that best describes the features of the plant in question so that you have a three-digit plant code.

Again, observation is key.

To determine the three-digit plant code, first ascertain if the plant you are trying to identify is a tree, shrub, or vine. Trees are upright plants with a main trunk and branches coming off of the main trunk. Shrubs are usually smaller in stature and have multiple stems instead of a main trunk. Vines are twining plants with thin stems that generally climb on the ground or other plants. From the key, choose the number (1, 2, or 3) that corresponds for your first digit.

Next, look at the leaf and branch arrangement. When the leaves or branches grow in circles around the stem, they are *whorled*; if they grow directly across from each other, they are *opposite*; when they are arranged singly on the stem one after the other, they are *alternate*. The second digit results from this observation.

Finally, look at a leaf (or a few to make sure that they are the same) and closely examine its edge. If the edge, or margin, of the leaf is unbroken with no ridges, edges, or teeth, it is considered *entire*. The term *with teeth* describes leaf edges with regular indentions. These distinctions are sometimes subtle, so look closely. *Lobes* are deep indentations in leaves (think of oak trees) that can be pointed or rounded. Divided or compound leaves have leaves divided into separate parts called leaflets. An example would be a clover or rose leaf. This last category of edges provides the third number for your plant code.

To use the key, take the three-numbered code that you created and use those three digits to identify the plant. Here's an example:

A maple would produce the following code. It is a tree (1), with opposite leaf/branch arrangement (1) that has pointed lobes (4). Thus, the code is 114, which corresponds with red maple. Voila! Sometimes it is not easy, so practice and you will get better at making these identifications. Remember, too, that not all island plants are represented here, especially nonnative yard and garden plants.

KEY TO WOODY PLANTS
Plant Habit

Trees usually have a single trunk and are tall. Shrubs are shorter and usually multistemmed. Vines have thin, flexible stems and twine around other plants.

Tree 1
Shrub 2
Vine 3

Leaf and Branch Arrangement

Opposite or whorled (circle around the stem) . . 1
Alternate 2

Leaf Edges

Entire 1
With teeth 2
Round lobes 3
Pointed lobes 4
Divided or compound 5

114 Red maple, *Acer rubrum.*

121 Beetlebung, *Nyssa sylvatica.*

121 Gray willow, *Salix cinerea.* Leaves long and narrow, base is rounded.

WITH FINE TEETH

122 Chokecherry, *Prunus virginiana.* Shrublike, leaves are egg-shaped, short-pointed, and sharply toothed.

122 Black cherry, *Prunus serotina.* Tree, bluntly toothed leaves. Edible fruit.

WITH COARSE TEETH

122 Beech, *Fagus grandifolia.*

122 Large-toothed poplar, *Populus grandidentata.*

122 Gray birch, *Betula populifolia.* With coarse and fine teeth.

122 Hawthorn, *Crataegus* spp. Teeth variable, species identification difficult.

123 White oak, *Quercus alba.* Lobes deeply cut, long and slender.

123 Post oak, *Quercus stellata*. Lobes often blunt or squarish, leaf usually leathery, shiny.

124 Black oak, *Quercus velutina*. Sinuses shallow.

124 Scarlet oak, *Quercus coccinea*. Sinuses deep and rounded.

124 Sassafras, *Sassafras albidum*. Leaves vary; some have no lobes, others have two or three.

125 Black locust, *Robinia pseudoacacia.* An introduced tree that has become common. The leaves are dull green and compound with as many as 19 oval leaflets.

211 Sheep laurel or **Lambkill,** *Kalmia angustifolia.* Evergreen shrub from one to two feet tall. Clusters of pink flowers around the stem with whorls of leaves below and above. Dried fruit often persists. Foliage poisonous to livestock. The shape of the flowers reveals this plant's relationship to **mountain laurel**, *Kalmia latifolia.*

211 Swamp azalea, *Rhododendrum viscosum.* Leaves and branches whorled.

212 Arrowwood, *Viburnum dentatum*. Coarsely toothed.

212 Marsh elder, *Iva frutescens*. Evenly toothed, lower leaves opposite.

221 Maleberry, *Lyonia ligustrina*. Fruit dry capsule.

221 Dangleberry, *Gaylussacia frondosa*. Leaves bluish-green.

221 Black huckleberry, *Gaylussacia baccata.* Yellowish-green, resin dots on back of leaves, spreads. Coastal plains plant, sunny places.

221 Highbush blueberry, *Vaccinium corymbosum.* Common on edges of wetlands.

WITH FINE TEETH

222 Lowbush blueberry, *Vaccinium angustifolium.* Leaves mostly narrow and finely toothed. Plant of coastal plains.

222 Sweet pepperbush, *Clethra alnifolia.* Leaf rough.

222 Black chokeberry, *Aronia melanocarpa.* Leaf smooth.

222 Smooth shadbush, *Amelanchier* spp. A large genus, *A. canadensis* is probably the most common on the Island. Bark smooth and mottled gray.

222 Winterberry, *Ilex verticillata.* Leaves sharply toothed, deciduous.

222 Beach plum, *Prunus maritima*. Edible purple fruits.

222 Northern bayberry, *Myrica pensylvanica*. Rounded teeth at tips, olive green, leaves fragrant when crushed, dry soil. Used for flavoring stews in colonial times.

222 Sweet gale, *Myrica gale*. Leaves with rounded teeth at tips, blue green, smaller than bayberry, leaves fragrant when crushed. Swamps and wetlands. Also used for flavoring.

WITH COARSE TEETH

222 Hazelnut, *Corylus americana*. Leaf stalk fuzzy.

222 Groundsel bush, *Baccharis halimifolia*. Fewer teeth, variable with rounded teeth.

222 Sweet fern, *Comptonia peregrina*. Dark green with rounded teeth.

222 Swamp rose mallow, *Hibiscus moscheutos*. Large pink blossoms in late summer.

222 Dwarf chestnut oak, *Quercus prinoides*. Leaf variable; teeth pointed or rounded.

224 Scrub oak, *Quercus ilicifolia*. Holly shaped.

225 Pasture rose, *Rosa carolina*. Leaves compound, stipules narrow, thorns straight.

225 Rugosa rose, *Rosa rugosa*. Leaflets dark and shiny, crinkled. Compound leaves. Not native.

225 Swamp rose, *Rosa palustris*. Prickles at base of petioles. Compound leaves.

225 Virginia rose, *Rosa virginiana*. Stipules broadly winged; thorns typically curved; stout, flowering branches without prickles. Leaves compound.

225 Multiflora rose, *Rosa multiflora.* Arching branches, usually seven to nine leaflets. Compound leaves. Invasive.

225 Elderberry, *Sambucus canadensis.* Usually five to 11 leaflets, sharply toothed.

225 Poison sumac, *Toxicodendron vernix.* Leaves compound, leaflets entire, flowers and fruits in loose clusters. Very poisonous.

225 Smooth sumac, *Rhus glabra.* Compound leaves, leaflets very sharply toothed.
225 Dwarf, shiny, or winged sumac, *Rhus copallina.* Compound leaves with winglike appendages along stems.
321 Bearberry, *Arctostaphylos uva-ursi.* Leaves evergreen, ground cover.

321 Common greenbrier, catbrier, bullbrier, *Smilax rotundifolia.* Sharp thorns, forms impenetrable thickets.

322 Climbing bittersweet, *Celastrus scandens.* Leaves finely toothed, flowers terminal clusters.

321 Asiatic bittersweet, *Celastrus orbiculatus*. Leaves blunt-toothed, nearly round, flowers in axils of leaves. Both *Celastrus* species highly invasive.
324 Grape. *Vitis* spp. Lobes with teeth.

325 Poison ivy. *Toxicodendron radicans*. Three leaflets. Serious irritant.

326 Virginia creeper, *Parthenocissus quinquefolia*. Palmately compound leaves with five leaflets.

327 Blackberry, *Rhubus allegheniensis*. Plant prickly all over.

REFERENCES

For more information about any of the trees and shrubs in this guide, see Elbert Little, *National Audubon Society Field Guide to North American Trees* (Knopf, 1980), and David Allan Sibley, *The Sibley Guide to Trees* (Knopf, 2009). George Petrides's *Field Guide to Trees and Shrubs* (Houghton Mifflin Harcourt, 1973) and George Symonds's *Tree Identification Book* (William Morrow, 1973) and *Shrub Identification Book* (William Morrow, 1973) also provide additional resources. Symonds's books use photographs of leaves, flowers, and bark to aid in identification.

CHAPTER FIVE

Pinkletink

A Guide to Island Fauna

In all things of nature there is something of the marvelous.

—Aristotle

The Island's flora represents species that have adapted to Island living, as we have. In some cases, they even differ from their mainland cousins. Chickadees are an example. The song of chickadees on the Island differ from those on the mainland. Isolation has its effects, another of which is the absence of breeding populations of fox, coyote, and other larger mammalian predators.

Fortunate for wildlife lovers, some species on the Island exist in few other places and some are at the edges of their range here. An example of the former is the northeastern tiger beetle, whose Vineyard population is one of the last remaining. Barn owls fall into the latter category, not usually found on the mainland, but surviving here due to mild temperatures. We are also blessed with birds that breed on our beaches, like the piping plover, terns, and oystercatcher that might be peeping next to us on a sunny summer day.

The diversity of some island animal groups can be astounding. Insects fall into this group. We were spared widespread DDT spraying and are lucky to have a robust diversity of invertebrates. Bees are a good example; in a recent study, more than 150 species of native bees were identified.

A description of the many wild things—native and washashore, aquatic and land-loving—follows to help you identify and appreciate the bounty of beings that share the island's lands and waters.

SPONGES Sponges are among the most primitive organisms and are in the phylum Porifera. They are strictly aquatic (water-loving), almost entirely marine (salt water), sedentary, and deceptively simple in appearance. Sponges are more frequently seen in tropical waters, although at least 10 species can be found around the Island.

Shells riddled with small holes are the most common evidence of local sponge activity. The **boring sponge**, *Cliona* spp., is responsible, as it has been for millions of years, for drilling into oysters and other mollusks. Occasionally, the brightly colored orange or yellow animal is seen encrusting shells. Another sponge that sometimes washes ashore during storms is the red- to yellow-colored **finger sponge**, also called **Mermaid's glove sponge**, *Haliclona oculata*, a bottom dweller from offshore.

JELLYFISH **Portuguese man-of-war**, *Physalia physalis*, is easily recognized, and with good reason: it is the most feared invertebrate of the Atlantic coast. Arriving as a summer-wind-driven vagrant, it periodically appears on the south shore. Though beautiful, the Portuguese man-of-war is a very dangerous animal whose sting is potent even days after it washes ashore. Bright blue or purple tinged with pink, grows over one foot long with tentacles to 50 feet.

Moon jellyfish, *Aurelia aurita*, can be found in brackish coastal ponds undulating while drifting with the currents. It is readily distinguished by the four-lobed mouth accentuated by four arc-shaped reproductive organs. The bell is fringed with short stinging hairs. Tiny individuals can be found in February, but as they mature and grow through summer and fall they become more obvious. Pale pink, orange, or milky white; grows up to 10 inches in diameter.

Lion's mane or red jellyfish, *Cyanea capillata*, is much larger in size than the moon jellyfish and possesses a greater array of long, stinging tentacles. Stripes of red, orange-brown, or purple radiate from the center; tentacles are reddish brown to yellowish, usually about one foot in diameter, but can reach more than eight feet in other areas.

Comb jellyfish or **ctenophores** are similar in appearance to the jellyfish listed above, though they are not true jellyfish. Comb jellies do not possess stinging apparatus, and they develop through simpler life stages. **Leidy's comb jelly**, *Mnemiopsis leidyi*, is the fragile, clear, bell-shaped comb jelly found floating freely in late summer in our brackish ponds. Its presence is best noted at night as they are wonderfully bioluminescent,

Portuguese man-of-war

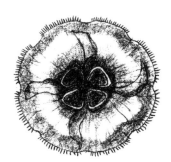

Moon jellyfish

TIPS FOR TRIPS

GET COMFORTABLE: To really enjoy field trips, prepare for your own comfort. Common sense should tell you what to wear and how much to carry. Better to travel lightly than to tote unnecessary gear. Use the following list for suggestions and as reminders:

- Insect repellent
- Sunscreen
- Comfortable footwear
- Hat for protection from the sun and to help keep insects away from the face
- Extra clothes, such as a sweater or windbreaker for added protection, particularly if you plan to be near the ocean or if inclement weather threatens

Also Consider

- Notebook for recording your experiences
- Field guides for your special interest to supplement the information in this guide.
- Binoculars
- Magnifying glass or hand lens
- Camera

glowing when the water is agitated or as they bump pilings, stones, and boats or even you during a nighttime swim. Clear and iridescent, up to six inches long.

CORALS, ANEMONES, AND HYDROIDS This phylum is better represented in warmer waters than in the sounds, bays, and harbors of the Vineyard. However, a few may be seen here.

Northern star coral, *Astrangia poculata*, is the only true coral here. It occurs from the low-water mark out to deeper waters as encrustations on stones and shells.

Orange-striped green anemone, *Duadumene luciae*, is a common anemone here. Imported from Japan, they are less than an inch in height, brown to olive-green. Their body column usually has longitudinal stripes of cream orange or yellow. These anemones are found on rocks and pilings in shallow water.

Frilled anemone, *Metridium senile*, can be found attached to pilings and rocks in the intertidal zone. It is a plankton eater. The **ghost anemone**, *Diadumene leucolena*, is much smaller and prefers protected waters.

Snail fur, *Hydractinia echinata*, is a fascinating and favorite hydroid. Snail fur takes its colonial form as an encrusting horny mat of organisms that covers shells, especially those of the flat-clawed hermit crab and other gastropods.

MOLLUSKS Perhaps one of the most familiar of large animal groups, mollusks include such varied animals as snails, clams, squid, and octopuses. Diverse as they may seem, each has a calcareous shell, ventral muscular foot, gut with two openings, and a body cavity.

When using this key you may want to carry a more comprehensive field guide as well. Unfortunately, a shell guide specific to the Vineyard that was written many years ago is now out of print. If you can locate a copy of *Exploring for Sea Shells on Martha's Vineyard* (Felix Neck Wildlife Trust, 1970) by Richards J. Heuer Jr., consider yourself very lucky. Another great marine guide is *A Field Guide to the Marine Life of Nantucket* (Maria Mitchell Association, 2001) by Jennifer Andrew and Inga Fredland.

Most of the shells included in this key can be found on our beaches. Each species tends to have places of concentration. Some are common in sheltered waters such as harbors and bays; others are found on the beaches of the sounds; still others only on south shore beaches. Some, like the common **Atlantic boat shell**, are ubiquitous. This list is by no means exhaustive, and you may find something not included here.

To identify shells, first consider whether they are snaillike (gastropod) or clamlike, with a two-hinged shell (pelecypod or bivalve). Gastropods include snails, limpets, and sea slugs. Snails are the most common representative of this group and live in a single-whorled shell, though some, like the aforementioned Atlantic boat shell, also called slipper snails, buck the trend. Slipper snails differ from other members of the snail family by having a raised deck inside and no whorls.

Clams are bivalves, which describes their two shells. Usually only a single hinge is seen. Bivalves are different from gastropods, which have whorls and lack a hinged joint. Mussels, oysters, arks, cockles, and scallops are included in the bivalve group along with clams.

To use the key below, create a three-number code by using the descriptions. First decide whether you have a gastropod or bivalve (1 or 2). Then decide whether the shell is round (1) or elongated (length two or more times the width) (2). Finally, determine the shell's overall length measured through its greatest dimension (1, 2, or 3). The resulting three-digit codes can be found with the illustrations that follow the key.

Each species of mollusk grows in size over the years, and specimens found of any one species can vary. Some may not fit neatly into the third category. They have been placed according to their ultimate size. A more complete shell guide can give you the range of sizes for each species.

Key to Mollusks

Gastropod (snail–like) **1**
Bivalve (clam–like). **2**

Shape:
Basically round **1**
Elongated **2**

Size:
Less than one inch. **1**
One to three inches **2**
More than three inches **3**

111 Common periwinkle, *Littorina littorea*, is abundant. It is found clinging to rocks and to the seaweed it feeds on. Periwinkles were introduced from Europe in 1850 and are edible.

111 Smooth periwinkle, *Littorina obtusata*, is yellow, orange, or brown. It lives on rockweed and hides under the plant's wet fronds when the tide is low.

111 Rough periwinkle, *Littorina saxatilis*, has a pointed spire, and the body whorls are rounded.

112 Common northern moon shell, *Lunatia heros*, is a voracious carnivore that preys on other mollusks and worms, and it also eats dead fish. Occasionally you can find its odd–looking sand collar egg case or its brown paisley-shaped operculum.

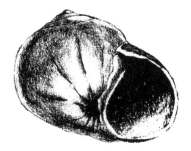

Northern moon snail

Operculum

112 Shark's eye, *Polinices duplicatus*, is similar to the northern moon shell, though much less common. It can be differentiated by looking at the umbilicus (the small hole next to the larger opening of the whorl). The umbilicus of the moon snail is open, while the shark's eye's umbilicus is closed off by a covering known as a callus.

112 Spotted northern moon shell, *Lunatia triseriata*, is much smaller than either of the other moon snails. It is sometimes seen at Squibnocket, Lambert's Cove, or along the south shore.

121 Atlantic oyster drill, *Urosalpinx cinerea*, is very common on many sound and harbor beaches; it is less common along the north shore. This predator of mollusks uses its radula (drilling tongue) to get into hard shells so that it can eat the soft animal inside.

121 Thick-lipped oyster drill, *Eupleura caudata*, is similar to the Atlantic oyster drill and may be distinguished by its more pointed vertical ribs and angled shoulder.

121 Well-ribbed dove shell, *Costoanachis translirata*, is not often found. They live on rocky or shelly bottoms. **121 Greedy dove shell**, *Costoanachis avara*, is similar to *C. translirata* but is relatively shorter and wider, and the body whorls are noticeably more rounded.

121 Eastern mud nassa or mud dog whelk, *Ilyanassa trivittata*, is a rather undistinguished shell; mature specimens become noticeably eroded. This snail feeds on detritus (dead decaying organic matter) on muddy bottoms.

121 New England nassa, *Nassarius atrivittatus*, has a beady surface caused by the intersection of spiral lines and longitudinal ridges. It is found around seaweed on sandy beaches, most commonly along the south shore.

122 Common Atlantic slipper or boat shell, *Crepidula fornicata*, is the most abundant shell found on Vineyard beaches. The "deck" inside the shell gives it its common name. As with many other species of invertebrates, especially those that lack mobility to seek out a mate, this snail changes sex as it grows—male when young, female when fully grown. They usually grow stacked one on top of another, thus the scientific name, with the females at the bottom. Edible.

122 Eastern white slipper, *Crepidula plana*, is similar in design, but flat and white.

123 Channeled whelk, *Busycon canaliculatum*, is a large snail that grows to seven inches long and is grooved next to the body whorl.

123 Knobbed whelk, *Busycon carica*, has "knobs" on the outer curve of the body whorl and is similar in size to the channeled whelk. **Waved whelks**, *Baccinum undataum*, can also be found, although they are half the size of the other whelks. Most interesting is their fist-sized egg case, which resembles large seeds stuck together.

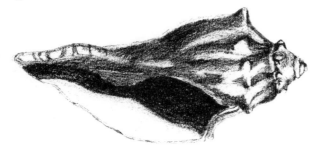

211 Jingle shell, *Anomia simplex*, is almost transparent, white, yellow, orange, or black, and can be quite brittle. When strung together, they make a bell-like sound, thus the name.

211 Morton's egg cockle, *Laevicardium mortoni*, is bright yellow inside when fresh; often marked with a darker splotch or pattern inside or outside or both.

211 Chestnut astarte, *Astarte castanea*, has a thick and solid shell and can be found along the south shore.

212 Transverse ark, *Anadara transversa*, is one of the three arks found on ocean beaches of the Vineyard. It can be distinguished from the others by the direction of the ribs when viewed horizontally. With this shell the ribs seem to point straight down.

212 Atlantic bay scallop, *Argopecten irradians*, is a Vineyard favorite. These shells come in a wide variety of colors and patterns, some of them developed by the Martha's Vineyard Shellfish Group, which grows and distributes bivalves for release into Island ponds. The round adductor muscle is the part Americans prefer to eat.

213 Northern quahog, *Merceneria mercenaria*, is the shell that the Native Americans used to make their noted purple wampum beads. Purple beads were worth twice as much as white wampum.

222 Blue mussel, *Mytilus edulis*, is the familiar edible mussel, blue in color, inside and out. The hinge is at the end of the shell.

222 Northern horse mussel, *Modiolus modiolus*, is similar to the blue mussel, different in the color of the periostracum (outer covering), which is brown, and in the hinge, which is off to one side. The interior is white and partially pearly, and it is larger than the other mussels.

222 Atlantic ribbed mussel, *Geukensia demissa*, is the same shape as the other mussels, but the surface is covered with numerous radiating ribs. The interior is iridescent.

222 False angel wing, *Petricola pholadiformis*, has a thin white shell that resembles the familiar true angel wings found in the South.

223 Eastern oyster, *Crassostrea virginica*, grows up to 10 inches in length. Specimens found on the beach normally range from one to five inches and can be highly variable in shape. Individual oysters are notable for their ability to filter up to 50 gallons of water per day.

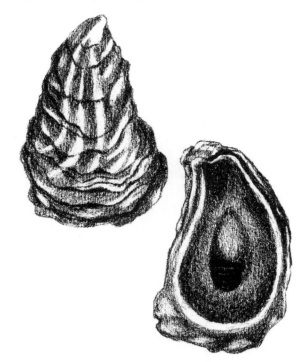

223 Common razor clam or Jackknife clam, *Ensis directus*, is shaped like an old-fashioned razor. Very shiny when not eroded. Edible, but hard to catch as they are vertical burrowers, able to dig themselves down more than three feet to avoid predators. Beware of their sharp shells.

223 Soft-shelled clam, *Mya arenaria*. One shell of each pair has a large, spoon-shaped projection at the hinge, perpendicular to the plane of the shell. They are usually chalky white. These clams, called steamers, long-necked, and Ipswich clams elsewhere, are edible and can be found in restaurants and fish markets. Town permits are required if you want to harvest clams, oysters, and other bivalves.

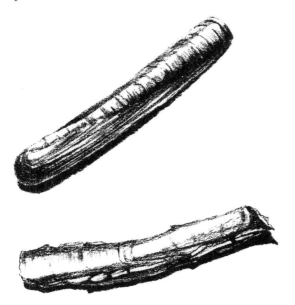

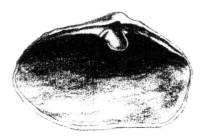

REFERENCES

Several good shell and shore references are readily available at local bookstores and libraries. An oldie but goodie is Richards Heuer's *Exploring for Sea Shells on Martha's Vineyard* (Felix Neck Wildlife Trust, 1970).

Compact and easy to carry is Tucker R. Abbott and George Sandstrom's *A Guide to the Identification of Seashells of North America* (Golden Guides, 2001).

Three other excellent books that provide a wealth of knowledge on marine animals include Deborah Coulombe's *A Seaside Naturalist* (Fireside, 1984); *A Field Guide to the Marine Life of Nantucket* (Maria Mitchell Association, 2001) by Jennifer Andrew and Inga Fredland; and Howard Weiss's *Marine Animals of Southern New England and New York* (Connecticut Geological and Natural History Survey, 1995).

ANNELIDS Generally small, long, and flattened, the flatworms include the freshwater planarians, which may be remembered from introductory biology classes.

Clam worm, *Alitta virens*, is often used as bait. It is a large, bright, iridescent marine worm and a good swimmer. These worms have powerful jaws and inflict a painful bite, as many anglers can attest. The mating habit of these worms is spectacular. At certain times, related to the phases of the moon, thousands of clam worms leave their burrows and meet to spawn in a spiraling swarm that goes on for hours.

Sinistral spiral tubeworm, *Spirobis spirobis*, is the most abundant worm of all and seldom noticed by people. They cement themselves in tiny coiled tubes to the blades of seaweeds and eelgrass and can be easily found in the wrack line debris.

The **lugworm**, *Arenicola* spp., is a feared or favorite worm, depending on your perspective. This marine worm deposits its eggs in a long, gelatinous mass that can be up to eight inches long and as thick as a cucumber. It is more common to see this mass, nicknamed "sea snot," due to its mucus-like look and feel.

ARTHROPODS This enormous and diverse phylum contains shrimps, crabs, lobsters, spiders, and insects—all sharing a basic body plan typified by the presence of jointed appendages, a hard exoskeleton, and external segmentation.

Crustaceans

This class contains fairy shrimp, barnacles, scuds, pillbugs, crabs, and others. Each is a gill breather with two antennae.

Barnacles: A few species are found locally, most of which are members of the genus Balanus and are the rock and piling-dwelling varieties. Louis Agassiz, one of the great 19th-century scientists, describes a barnacle as a "shrimplike animal, standing on its head in a limestone house and kicking food into its mouth with its feet." The more exotic goose barnacles (*Lepas* spp.) are stalked and pelagic, arriving on debris found on our south shore in summer.

Goose barnacles

Common shore or grass shrimp, *Palaemonetes vulgaris*, are abundant in all the sandy and muddy beaches of the Vineyard. They are hard to see but easy to catch if you drag a net along rocks and seaweeds at the shoreline. You may be aware of them when they tickle your toes when you wade in shallow water at low tide. The sand shrimp resembles a miniature lobster and grows to a maximum of two inches. Its coloration is speckled gray on a beige body.

Sand shrimp, *Crangon semptemspinosa*, tend to be lighter in color than the grass shrimp, appearing translucent, although they can change color and become darker to camouflage themselves. They flex the muscles in their tail, which makes them jump.

American lobster, *Homarus americanus*, when alive, is dark green in color, blotched with blue and reddish markings. The coloration is darker on top and lighter and yellowish below. Sometimes blue lobsters are found, though these are rare. Lobsters are scavengers and their diet includes other lobsters; fish, dead or alive; eelgrass; seaweeds; or whatever else they can get their claws on.

Mole crab, *Emerita talpoida*, is one of the few animals adapted to life in the turbulent swash-and-backwash community, the part of the beach where the waves wash in and out. Hard to see and harder to catch alive, look for a pale tan to gray streamlined shell about three-quarters of an inch long in the wrack line on any ocean-facing beach.

Hermit crab, *Pagurus* spp., will always be a renter, but never an owner. It lives in empty shells, frequently seeking a new home. Hermit crabs often explore empty shells and sometimes try them on for size. If the shell fits well, the crab stays with its new portable home; otherwise it scuttles back to its old home. Although they look like a true member of the crustacean clan in front—menacing claws and hard outer skeleton—they are unarmored and defenseless from behind. The borrowed shell is used to protect their soft abdomen. Two species, the **long-clawed hermit crab**, *Pagurus longicarpus*, and the **flat-clawed hermit crab**, *Pagurus pollicaris*, are most often found.

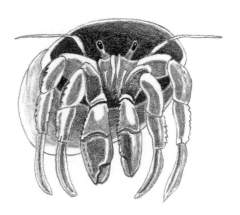

Blue crab, *Callinectes sapidus*, belongs to the group of swimming crabs. The back legs are flattened, paddle-like, permitting them to swim. In fact, this crab's scientific name means "beautiful swimmer." The distinctive shell with spikes projecting sideways is blue. When it molts (sheds its hard shell), it is the soft-shell crab that is considered such a delicacy.

Green crab, *Carcinus maenas*, is a scavenger. The dark-green squarelike carapace is seen during the day and at night, as it is constantly searching for dead fish and decaying matter. This aggressive crab is not native and has invaded native crab habitat, outcompeting the locals and leading to their decline. Another invasive crab is the **Japanese shore crab**, *Hemigrapsus sanguineus*. It is smaller than the green crab and can be identified by its bands of purple and yellow on its legs.

Atlantic mud crab, *Panopeus herbstii*, is a dark crab with black or brown tips on its claws. Although small in size, it is pugnacious and can capture and eat fiddler crabs.

Marsh fiddler crab, *Uca pugnax*, lives in holes at the edge of the marsh. Look for these holes, often with small mud pellets just outside, and watch for the male— easily identified with one claw significantly larger than the other.

Lady crab, *Ovalipes ocellatus*, also called a **calico crab** because of its patterned carapace, is known for its aggressive behavior and sharp claws. Handle with care if at all.

Fiddler crab

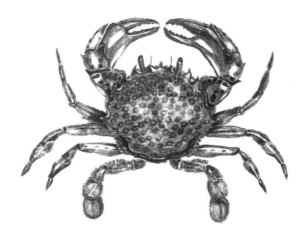

Lady crab

Spider crab, *Libinia emarginata*, is long-legged with a spiny carapace that is also called a **decorator crab**. Their claws are small, so their only defense against predators (gulls and fish) is the camouflage of algae that often cover the tops of their shells. Watch them eat algae picked from off of their own shell.

Shame-faced crab, *Calappa flammea*, is a crab not often seen. This light brownish–red rounded crab appears to be hiding its face using its claws.

Sand hoppers, *Americorchestia longicornis* and *Orchestia agilis*, are amphipods, close relatives of crabs and shrimps, not insects.

ARACHNIDS This class of animals includes spiders, mites, and ticks. Few groups are as common, wide-ranging, or poorly understood as these. Literally millions of individual spiders can be found in any marsh, field, or forest. Living on the ground or burrowing, the **wolf spiders** are very common, as are the familiar **garden spiders** and the numerous sheet and funnel web spinners so noticeable in the morning dew.

Wolf spider, members of the *Lycosidae* family, are hunters who run down their prey rather than trapping them in webs. The female lives in a hole, frequently in the dunes under a beach pea, tending her young while the male hunts at night for their food. They are also found in the woods, fields, and most any habitat and are notable for their large size and hairy appearance.

Garden spider, *Argiope* spp., is notable for its yellow and black body and unique zigzag patterned web.

Two spiders that are often asked about due to their venomous and painful bites are the **northern black widow**, *Latrodectus variolus*, and **brown recluse**, *Loxosceles reclusa*. Though the black widow spider can be found on the Island, it is very scarce and rarely seen by people. Brown recluse spiders are not native to the Island; they are a more southern species that is occasionally imported to our area in produce or plant material.

Horseshoe crab, *Limulus polyphemus*, is a living fossil found only along the American Atlantic coast. It has no extant close relatives, although it is distantly related to spider mites. Possessing ten legs, ten booklike gills, a long telson (tail), and primitive eyes, the horseshoe crab serves as an important research animal as well as a glimpse of primitive arthropod characteristics. In late spring horseshoe crabs come ashore to mate during the full and new moon. The females lay eggs and bury them at the high-tide line along the shoreline of some of our beaches and ponds.

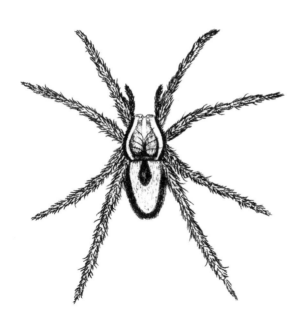

Wolf spider

Garden spider

American dog tick or **wood tick**, *Dermacentor variabilis*, has an oval, dark, thick-skinned body. The male has a white-marked shield over all its back; the female has only half of its body covered. With eight legs and measuring about three-sixteenths of an inch, it shouldn't be missed. This tick caries Rocky Mountain spotted fever and tularemia. Always check yourself for this and other ticks.

Deer tick, *Ixodes dammini*, similar in shape, but much smaller. Although tiny, it carries Lyme disease (see Tips for Trips, page 25), babesiosis, and anaplasmosis, all tick-borne illnesses to be avoided.

The **Lone Star tick** also has been identified on Martha's Vineyard and it carries ehrlichiosis. Always do tick checks.

INSECTS More living things belong to this class than to any other taxonomic division, since they are adapted to finding a niche in nearly every available environment. A few have managed to overcome the hazards of salinity, but most are fresh water and terrestrial. A small fraction are adept at exploiting our blood and horticultural endeavors and therefore have drawn attention out of proportion to their actual numbers and importance. Those less obnoxious in their ways can provide more puzzles and satisfying inquiries than any one life span would allow.

Dog tick

Deer tick

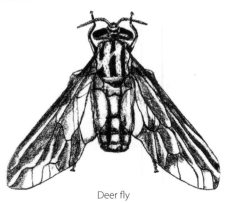

Deer fly

The remarkable diversity of habitat types occurring on the Vineyard is reflected in the diversity of insect species in residence. The Vineyard is lucky to have avoided the historical widespread spraying of DDT. What follows is a very brief introduction to some hexapodous (six-legged) denizens of the Island.

Aquatics

Although there are a very large number of insect species, only a small percentage of all insects are aquatic. Some pass only the egg and larval stages submerged. Others depend upon an aqueous medium for their entire lives.

Mayflies, stoneflies, caddisflies, dragonflies, and several true flies have aquatic larval stages and live a longer time in the underwater realm than as conspicuous flying adults.

Several species of Vineyard dragonflies are likely to be encountered while out and about.

Near any pond from mid-August to November, **meadowhawks**, the stunning crimson members of the genus Sympetrum, will be flying. They are not terribly shy and avail themselves readily to any observer desiring an effortless lesson in dragonfly behavior.

In September, swarms, numbering in the thousands, of migratory **green darners**, *Anax junius*, hunt insects above fields in the outwash plains gathering fuel for their

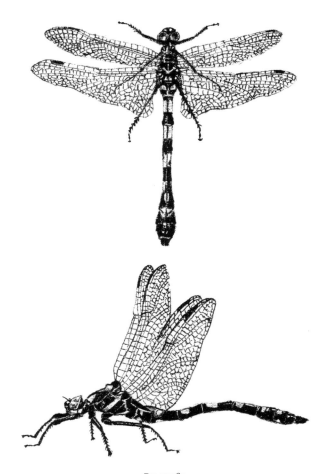

Dragonfly

journey south. Contrary to a common misconception, dragonflies are not capable of stinging anything.

On any day between May and August, the more fragile and diminutive damselflies are seen. Differentiate them from the dragonflies by looking at their wings at rest; dragonflies hold their wings out to the sides, while damselflies hold their wings back behind them

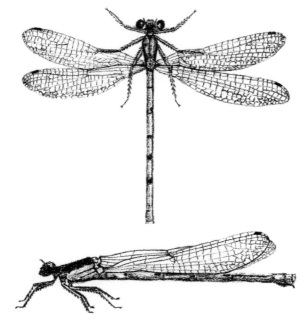

Damselfly

and directly over their bodies. **Bluets**, the metallic blue and black members of the genus Enallagma, are particularly attractive. They fly close to the ground and out of the wind.

Near dusk or dawn in the summer months, swarms of mayflies, caddisflies, and stoneflies emerge from the water and rather clumsily fly for the first time. Usually they stay close to fresh water.

Most larval caddisflies seek protection by enclosing themselves in elaborate cases. Different kinds use different materials in construction, employing pine needles, leaves, twigs, and sand. Some crawl slowly, browsing on algae, while others are capable of unexpectedly rapid movement. A small disk of sand suddenly scooting along a pond bottom is certain to be a caddisfly.

Entirely aquatic hemipterans, or true bugs, reside in all levels of our ponds and streams. At the surface the **water striders**, *Gerris* spp., spend their lives feeding on other insects that fall into the water. Water striders converge on anything that creates gentle ripples, which is easily demonstrated if one gently taps the water surface with the tip of a thin twig.

The closely related **water boatmen**, *Hesperocorixa* spp., and **back swimmers**, *Notonecta* spp., each have paddlelike legs and, aided by their streamlined shapes, row through the water beneath the surface. Water boatmen swim head down and feed upon the fluids of plants that they pierce. Swimming head up, the back swimmers use more rigid mouth parts for piercing the tissues of other animals.

The larger members of the aquatic Hemiptera, **giant water bugs**, *Belostoma* spp., and **water scorpions**, *Nepa* spp., are both predaceous and capable of seizing relatively large prey with their long forelegs. Although the long abdominal appendage of the water scorpion appears intimidating, it is used for breathing. However, all the predatory hemipterans should be handled with caution because their mouthparts are capable of piercing human skin.

The **beetles**, Coleoptera, also have both herbivorous and carnivorous members. Large and small **predaceous diving beetles**, *Dytiscidae* spp., of various genera are represented on the Vineyard. The larvae called **water tigers** have insatiable appetites. Many of the less active common beetles can also be observed or netted in shallow waters, and some come to lights.

No summary of aquatic Coleoptera can neglect mentioning the **whirligig beetles**, *Dineutes* spp. Their eyes are halved, enabling vision in water and air. Watch a group of these beetles for a few moments and observe their superior evasive tactics. It is difficult to follow one of them as it performs endless gyrations. As danger approaches, whole groups will disappear beneath the surface. Should a predator somehow manage to seize one of them, the beetle will secrete a powerful, foul-tasting chemical.

Water strider

Water boatman

Whirligig beetles

Terrestrial Insects

Prominent terrestrial Vineyard insects include 70 species of butterflies, more than 150 bee species, perhaps 1,800 beetles, and 1,300 moths. If you add to these unknown numbers of species of other orders, such as ants, wasps, true bugs, and grasshoppers, your list very quickly grows long.

Butterflies. Dark brown-black with pale yellow borders, the **mourning cloak butterfly**, *Nymphalis antiopa*, overwinters beneath bark and announces the first warm March days with its flight. A few weeks later, **Juvenals duskywing**, *Erynnis juvenalis*, brown with tiny clear wingspots, can be seen along dirt roads.

The caterpillars feed on oak leaves, and the adults emerge coincidently with the flowering of blueberry and huckleberry, from which they sip nectar. The season also brings **spring azures**, *Celastrina ladon*, and the ever present **cabbage white**, *Pieris rapae*.

In summer, the large **wood nymph**, *Cercyonis pegala*, with its prominent pair of eyespots will be seen nearly everywhere.

A few **monarchs**, *Danaus plexippus*, will be seen after they emerge from their chrysalises, but in the fall, during migration, they are far more common. At about the same time, the **viceroy**, *Limenitis archippus*, famous

Tiger Swallowtail

Spicebush Swallowtail

mimic of the monarch, can be differentiated from the monarch from a distance by its less leisurely flight.

Another mimic-model is the **red spotted purple**, *Limenitis arthemis*, a more abundant ornament of our summer days. Its model is the poisonous **pipevine swallowtail**, *Battus philenor*, whose caterpillars feed upon the vines from which they derive their name. Formerly only a straggler to the Island, the cultivation of pipevines has added to the range expansion of this butterfly. Other swallowtails, sulphurs, checkerspots, skippers, buckeyes, and painted ladies are also at home on the Island.

Nocturnal Insects

A warm summer night is a great time to gain an appreciation for the richness of the Island's insect fauna. Many moths that occur on the Island are rare or do not occur elsewhere in New England. Some of them are particularly good indicators of rare habitat. The large saturniid moths are the most spectacular. Huge, tailed, pale green, elegant in appearance, although less than graceful in flight, the **luna moth**, *Actias luna*, frequently visits windows and porch lights in July.

The **imperial moth**, *Eacles imperialis*, colored like speckled pancake batter, reaches the northern limit of

Monarch

Red Spotted Purple

Underwing moth

Luna moth

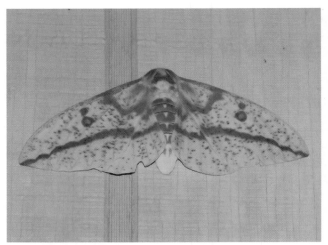

Imperial moth

its distribution on the Island. Smaller, with similar coloration and with the addition of two large eyespots on the hindwings, is the **io moth**, *Automeris io*. None of these are capable of feeding as adults. All the energy required for flying and mating is stored by the large caterpillars, which often attain lengths of two or more inches before overwintering.

There are many other attractive and intriguing insects of the Vineyard night. These would include numerous **underwing moths**, *Catocala* spp.; **tiger moths**, *Grammia* spp., *Apantesis* spp.; **fireflies**, *Lampyridae* spp.; and the large window-thudding **June bugs**, *Phyllophaga* spp., to name only a few.

Other Insects

On the shores of ponds and at the beach, along grassy roads and gravel pits, are the habitats of the attractive **tiger beetles**, Cicindelinae. More than half a dozen species are known to occur on the Vineyard. Some abundant, others quite rare, they can be seen running or flying with terrific speed. Voracious predators, they will overcome and devour any small creature less agile at scurrying across the sand.

There are many others, including click, long-horned, metallic-wood boring, and lady beetles; Orthopterans, crickets and their allies; mound-building ants, *Formica*

exsectoides; digger wasps of fields and dunes; hunters of grasshoppers and spiders; and also ant-loving and bee-parasitic beetles, both more typical of the Southwest but having representatives here.

ECHINODERMS **Common starfish** or **sea star**, *Asterias rubens*, is sometimes found washed up on the beach. This sea star usually has five blunt arms and is light orange to dark purple in color with a bright orange madreporite (a sieve plate in the center to bring in water). Each arm has rows of hollow feet on the lower side of its arms, each with rows of suckers at the tips. The sea star moves by extending its arms, attaching the suckers, and then contracting the arms. The feet also fasten around clams and exert pressure that will open the shell, allowing the sea star to feed.

Tiger beetle

Click beetle

Brittle sea stars, *Ophiopholis aculeata*, can be found in shallow waters on muddy bottoms or sheltered in clumps of mussels. Its arms are slender and dark. It eats worms and other small marine creatures.

The **sea urchin**, *Strongylocentrotus droebachiensis*, is uncommon in Vineyard waters. The live animals are covered with spines, but if any evidence of the sea urchin is found, it is the round shell (called a test), identified by its striking star-shaped pattern. Their usual diet is seaweed, although they sometimes eat small mussels.

Sand dollar, *Echinarachnius parma*, is another uncommon animal found rarely (at Lobsterville Beach, if at all). It is a flattened version of the sea urchin, thickly covered with short spines.

VERTEBRATES

Fish

Fish are well-covered in an old pamphlet titled *The Fishes of Martha's Vineyard* by Joseph B. Elvin, if you can find it. Copies may be available at the Martha's Vineyard

Common sea star

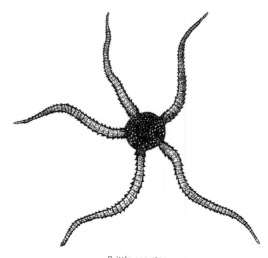

Brittle sea star

Museum and Island libraries. Fish are not covered in this guide, although the following books will provide species identification and information.

REFERENCES

Robins, C. R., C. C. Ray, and J. Douglas. *A Field Guide to Atlantic Coast Fishes: North America* (Houghton Mifflin Harcourt, 1999).

Weiss, Howard M. *Marine Animals of Southern New England and New York* (State Geological and Natural History Survey of Connecticut, 1995).

AMPHIBIANS

Salamanders

Salamanders originated in the Americas. The **eastern newt**, *Notophthalmus viridescens*, is extremely abundant on mainland New England but not so common on the Vineyard. In the moraine, a few populations occur.

Most newts spend part of their lives entirely terrestrial in a bright orange eft stage. Extremely poisonous to any predator, newts have bright coloration to advertise their protection. Typically newts undergo a complex metamorphosis consisting of aquatic egg and larval stages followed by a land-dwelling eft stage, which is followed by a return to water for an aquatic adult reproductive stage. When conditions are less than favorable, as in coastal areas, they are capable of a great deal of variation on this theme, eliminating part or all of these stages.

Woodland salamander, *Plethodon cinereus*, displays two principal color phases: the red-backed and the lead-backed. Combinations of the two phases are also encountered. This is the most abundant salamander in the Northeast. They can be found beneath boards just behind the dunes, but they are more common in the leaf litter and beneath logs in the woods. Although

Woodland salamander

requiring moisture, this salamander is entirely terrestrial. Eggs are laid in cavities beneath stones and logs and tended by the female.

Four-toed salamander, *Hemidactylium scutatum*, is the rarest of the Vineyard salamanders. Confined to sphagnum bogs in the moraine, only one locality has been verified on the Island (West Tisbury). Unmistakable when encountered, this small animal has four toes on the hind feet, is four-and-a-half inches long, and has a white belly with contrasting ink-black speckles and a conspicuous constriction at the base of the tail. The dorsal surface is usually reddish-brown.

Spotted salamander, *Ambystoma maculatum*, is also very rare and local, known only in a site in Edgartown.

Frogs

Green frog, *Rana clamitans*, is the frog you often see or hear (*gunk, gunk*), and usually around ponds as they tend to stay by water while the other Vineyard frogs spread out into the woods after the breeding season. They often are brown, but usually there is some green visible, and the male shows bright yellow coloring on its chin and throat and has a large ear drum (tympanum). They are about four inches long.

Bullfrog, *Rana catesbeiana*, is not welcome to our eyes or ears. This now common frog was introduced

less than 25 years ago and is present throughout the Island. Listen for its *jug o' rum* call.

Pickerel frog, *Rana palustris*, is boldly patterned. The **leopard frog**, *Rana pipiens*, can be confused with this species, but its spots are fewer and smaller and more of the ground color shows. Look for these frogs in woodland wetlands in the summertime.

The **eastern spadefoot**, *Scaphiopus holbrooki*, is almost certainly a resident, although sightings are few. It spends nearly its entire life burrowed in the ground, emerging to breed only after torrential spring rains. Years may pass without the proper conditions for emergence. Unlike other members of the anurans, the tadpoles achieve adulthood very quickly, usually only a matter of several days. Greenish-brown, the spadefoot usually possesses two pale lines on the back. Attaining only two to three inches in length and having a spade-like structure on each hind foot, this animal is very rare.

Spring peeper or **pinkletink**, *Pseudacris crucifer*, is a small brown to pinkish, disc-toed frog that is heard from early March throughout the breeding season. There is always a great contest each March to be the first to report hearing them to the local newspapers. They are abundant creatures and easily found when breeding but harder to find during the summer when their mating calls cease.

Toads

"All toads are frogs, but not all frogs are toads." If you are looking for frogs, West Tisbury is the best area to explore, according to Skip Lazell, author of *This Broken Archipelago* (Quadrangle, 1976), a reference to the reptiles and amphibians of this area. Be careful in handling frogs as many secrete noxious substances that can be very irritating, particularly if you should rub your eyes after touching one.

Here on the Vineyard, you can tell toads from frogs because toads' skins look dry, their faces are blunt, and their hind legs small by comparison with those of frogs, which have wet-looking skin, rather pointed heads, and heavy hind legs. These variations are different in other places.

Fowler's toad, *Bufo fowleri*, and **American toad**, *Bufo americanus*, are two very similar but rare toads found on the Island. If you find a toad and want to identify it, refer to Lazell's book. He describes how to score the differences in characteristics. You can content yourself with a fairly sure identification by noting the habitat in which you find a toad. Fowler's toad is found in sandy, open areas, even behind sand dunes. The American toad lives in the morainal woodlands of Up-Island.

Pickerel frog

Pinkletink

Fowler's toad

Snapping turtle

Painted turtle

REPTILES

Turtles

Snapping turtle, *Chelydra serpentina*, is the largest of the turtles found on the Vineyard. Although 30 pounds is large nowadays, there are records of snappers weighing 80 pounds. They may live as long as 25 years. Their shells are dark, with three broken ridges of coarse scales on the back. A border row of scales gives it a notched edge to the rear of the shell. Although this turtle moves slowly over the ground, it can reach out very rapidly with its head. Although not aggressive, they are better left alone as they can and will attack if provoked and their jaws are quite powerful. They have a long neck that extends to a surprising distance when ready to strike.

Painted turtle, *Chrysemys picta*, is found in both freshwater and brackish wetlands. The red markings that can be seen on the bottom edge of the carapace and its dark top show local variations. They grow up to eight inches in size.

Spotted turtle, *Clemmys guttata*, is smaller than the painted turtle and somewhat similar. It is quickly identified by the bright yellow spots on its dark carapace.

Eastern box turtle, *Terrapene carolina*, is notable for its high-arched carapace and generally dark brown shell blotched with yellow. A hinge on the front of the lower shell closes tightly. It eats insects and garden pests.

Sea turtles can be seen in our waters, migrating between their nesting areas in the south and their feeding areas in the north. **Green** (*Chelonia mydas*), **loggerhead** (*Caretta caretta*), **Kemp's Ridley** (*Lepidochelys kempii*), and **Atlantic leatherback** (*Dermochelys coriacea*) turtles can be seen in our waters. Occasionally during the late fall, some of these species can become cold-stunned or stranded, unable to move or swim. If you find a turtle alive or dead, please contact Mass Audubon's Felix Neck Wildlife Sanctuary at 508.627.4850 for assessment and information that could help save these turtles or provide information for ongoing sea turtle research.

Eastern box turtle

Snakes

Black racer or **black snake**, *Coluber constrictor*, may grow to six feet in length and is seen more often in the moraine than elsewhere. It will strike readily and rattle its tail in leaves very convincingly. Unfortunately they are often killed for such fine performances. The bite is not venomous.

Green snake, *Opheodrys vernalis*, is closely related to the black racer, but is smaller—usually less than two feet and bright green. Some have grayish or olive-green coloration. They are primarily insectivores.

Milk snake or **king snake**, *Lampropeltis triangulum*, is a colorful, boldly patterned species that feeds on rats, mice, and other snakes. It is smaller than the black snake and is not venomous.

Ringneck snake, *Diadophis punctatus*, is a dark snake with a yellow or orange-ish belly and a complete ring around its neck. Rare in the outwash plain, but more frequent in the moraine.

Milk snake

Ribbon snake, *Thamnophis sauritus*, is an active, agile, and attractive snake with bold stripes. It can reach three feet in length and feeds on fish, frogs, and salamanders.

Garter snake, *Thamnophis sirtalis*, is very common and differs in coloration and behavior in this region from other places, another example of the uniqueness of our animal populations. This snake is known to bite, so handling is not advised.

Red-bellied snake, *Storeria occipitomaculata*, is rarely seen on the Vineyard. Its coloration is somewhat variable, but usually it is brown to gray with a bright red belly, and is about a foot long.

The definitive reference on amphibians and reptiles for the Island and Cape Cod is James D. Lazell Jr., *This Broken Archipelago* (Quadrangle, 1976).

BIRDS Of the animals possessing backbones, the birds are the group about which we know the most, but even they pose many unanswered questions concerning details of their lives, distributions, and nesting status on the Island. Scientists continue to fill these gaps with banding and other ornithological research projects.

The National Audubon Society and books by Peterson, Sibley, and Crossely are all excellent resources for birders.

For more local knowledge, *Vineyard Birds II* by Susan Whiting and Barbara Pesch (Vineyard Stories, 2007) is the best reference to the species that have been sighted on the Island. Follow the bird and nature columns in the *Vineyard Gazette* and *Martha's Vineyard Times* for current information, as well as the Facebook group Martha's Vineyard Bird Alert for up-to-the-minute sightings.

Pressures from increasing human population and activities are stressing the nesting habits of many species, notably piping plovers, least terns, and other

Osprey

ground-nesting birds. Be aware of and heed posted shorebird signs on the beaches, and keep dogs on leashes and cats indoors to do your part to protect birds and their habitats.

The story of the successful efforts to increase populations of **osprey**, *Pandion haliaetus*, deserves mention. Natural nesting sites for ospreys—old, dead trees—are rare on the Vineyard, and telephone poles, often with transformers, were frequently selected as substitutes. Through the work of Gus Ben David, the first director of the Felix Neck Wildlife Sanctuary, and the help of a large crew of volunteers, sufficient numbers of poles were erected around the Island to provide safe nesting sites. From a population of a few nesting pairs in 1969, there are now about 70 nesting pairs of osprey on Martha's Vineyard.

REFERENCES

Bull, John, and John Farrand. *National Audubon Society Field Guide to North American Birds: Eastern Region* (Knopf, 1994).

Crossley, Richard. *The Crossley ID Guide* (Princeton University Press, 2011).

Gillespie, Mabel. *Where the Birds Are* (Tashmoo Press, 1976).

Peterson, Roger Tory. *A Field Guide to the Birds* (Houghton Mifflin, 2010).

Sibley, David Allen. *The Sibley Field Guide to Birds of Eastern North America* (Knopf, 2003).

Whiting, Susan B., and Barbara P. Pesch. *Vineyard Birds II* (Vineyard Stories, 2007).

MAMMALS The status of the mammals of Martha's Vineyard has changed over the years. Fossil records and midden piles provide evidence of species that no longer exist. Mammal populations have been manipulated more fully and more often by humans than any other class of animals.

Some have been exterminated, others introduced, and some reintroduced. In 1966 Allan Keith produced a pamphlet titled *The Mammals of Martha's Vineyard*, published by the Dukes County Historical Society, now the Martha's Vineyard Museum, though it is long out of print. The Felix Neck Wildlife Trust printed an article by Gwilyn S. Jones and Karen Driscoll in its 1979 *Naturalist* that listed and keyed the mammals of Martha's Vineyard. Only a few copies remain.

More recently, Allan Keith and Stephen Spongberg have compiled a book that provides much information about current and historic mammal species here. *Island Life: A Catalog of the Biodiversity on and around Martha's Vineyard* (Marine Biological Laboratories, 2008) now fills an important role in documenting Island species of flora and fauna.

Shrews and Moles

Shrews are small animals, the size of mice or smaller. They all have pointed noses, thick velvety fur, inconspicuous ears, tiny eyes, and chestnut-colored teeth. They are very active feeders.

On Martha's Vineyard, the **short-tailed shrew**, *Blarina brevicauda*, is abundant. They are extremely aggressive, prey on almost anything they can overcome, and are capable of killing prey as large as young rabbits. Short-tailed shrews possess a venomous bite, unique among mammals.

Masked shrew, *Sorex cinereus*, is uncommon on the Island. It has a coat of grayish-brown; the tail is longer than *Blarina*, partially hairy and bicolored. The more pointed nose readily distinguishes this species. The masked shrew consumes more than its own weight in food daily.

Eastern mole, *Scalopus aquaticus*, is abundant. The presence of these moles is detected by the long, sinuous, ground-level tunnels they create while searching for their favorite food, earthworms.

Bats

Little brown bat, *Myotis lucifugus*, is usually seen at dusk feeding on insects over ponds and fields. It is three to four inches long with an eight- to 10-inch wingspan. It roosts in attics and barns.

Red bat, *Lasiurus borealis*, is larger than the little brown bat and is red in coloration. It is a tree-roosting species that migrates south for the winter.

Two other bats, **Keen's myotis**, *Myotis keenii*, and **Hoary bat**, *Lasiurus cinereus*, have been mentioned in the historical record, though both are uncommon. Little is known about the bats that live on the Island, and concerns are being raised about white-nose syndrome, a disease that is decimating bat populations. One should be cautious about handling any individual bats, particularly disabled ones, as they can be infected with rabies.

Rabbits

Eastern cottontail, *Sylvilagus floridanus*, is an introduced game species and is found throughout the Island. The native **New England cottontail**, *Sylvilagus transitionalis*, former resident, is extinct on the Island because of the competition from the imported species. Its

Masked shrew

population suffered severely in the 1920s because of an epidemic disease probably introduced by the eastern cottontail.

Rodents

Eastern chipmunk, *Tamias striatus*, can be seen in wooded areas of the moraine, especially around stone walls.

Gray squirrel, *Sciurus carolinensis*, is abundant and frequently seen wherever there are trees.

White-footed mouse, *Peromyscus leucopus*, is particularly plentiful in wooded areas and often found

Eastern cottontail

around buildings. The ears are large, and the fur is reddish brown on the back, white underneath and on the feet.

Meadow vole, *Microtus pennsylvanicus*, has a heavy coat and is dark brown to chestnut in color. Its tail is relatively short. Because meadow voles are abundant, they serve as an important food source for hawks and owls.

Muskrat, *Ondatra zibethicus*, is somewhat common in and around freshwater or brackish ponds, marshes, and swamps. Dens constructed of cattails and reeds might be mistaken for those of beavers, which are not found on the Island. The muskrat is about two feet long with a tail that extends about a foot. Dark brown in color, a good field mark is its laterally compressed tail.

Norway rat, *Rattus norvegicus*, is abundant and was introduced with the colonists. Its fur is a coarse gray-brown, the eyes small and black, the ears prominent, and the tail scaly. They are efficient burrowers. They eat almost anything, reproduce rapidly in times when food is abundant, and can become a serious problem, as they are disease carriers.

Jumping mice are readily distinguished by their long tails and powerful hind legs. They are generally docile. Unlike the animals described above, they are true hibernators.

Meadow jumping mouse, *Zapus hudsonius*, is common although infrequently seen. They are active for only five or six months a year, when they are frequently preyed upon by hawks and owls. Seven to 10 inches in length, including tail, they have yellowish-brown fur on top with a darker dorsal stripe, white beneath.

Carnivores

Raccoon, *Procyon lotor*, is also known from remains in Wampanoag kitchen middens. The state Division of Fisheries and Game records indicate that populations were exterminated or dwindled over the years. It is rumored that a few were released here in the 1960s and the population has grown. They are quite extensive in their range and are a threat to domestic fowl and other wild ground-nesting birds.

Striped skunk, *Mephitus mephitis*, has a similar history to the raccoon. According to Allen Keith, the original species was known as the "star skunk," because it had a white spot on its head and on the tip of its tail. The usual white stripe on the back was either missing or very slender. Its unusual markings made its pelt particularly valuable, which probably caused its extinction. However, it is back with a vengeance. An avid egg hunter, skunks contribute to the decline of ground-nesting birds as well as snakes and turtles.

River otter, *Lontra canadensis*, is seen near water, although it roams widely. It is larger and sleeker than the muskrat, and its heavy, fur-covered tail also sets it apart. A graceful, playful, and strong swimmer, this animal is a delight to watch.

Domestic cat, *Felis catus*, is included here as there are feral cats—cats born in the wild to stray or wild cats—that never have been domesticated. They fill the niche of another truly wild cat, the bobcat, which was apparently exterminated after the first Europeans settled on the Island. They are an important factor in populations of ground-nesting birds and small avian species and have been known to kill small rabbits. Controlling feral cat populations and keeping cats indoors will go a long way to protecting birds.

River otter

Coyotes, *Canis latrans*, deserve a mention. While these animals are confirmed as close as the Elizabeth Islands and one was found dead on a Vineyard beach, only a few credible sightings have been reported. Likely there is at least one animal on the Island, but not a viable breeding population.

Deer

Fallow deer, *Dama dama*, were introduced to the Island as early as 1932, although it is likely the population no longer exists.

White-tailed deer, *Odocoileus virginianus*, are abundant and growing in numbers due to the increase in its preferred habitat—woodlands—and because of the declining interest in hunting. Deer numbers are now a concern because of its role in the increase of deer tick populations and the related prevalence of Lyme and other tick-borne diseases.

Marine Mammals

All marine mammals are protected by federal and state laws, including the Marine Mammal Protection and Endangered Species Acts. Harassing any live animal or collecting any part of a dead one is illegal. Contact Felix Neck Wildlife Sanctuary at 508.627.4850 to report live, stranded, or dead marine mammals.

Cetaceans—whales, porpoises, and dolphins. Many whales, dolphins, and porpoises are sighted in the waters around the Island, and an occasional animal washes ashore. **Common** and **white-sided dolphins**, *Delphinus delphis* and *Lagenorhynchus actutus*, respectively, can occasionally be seen. **Pilot**, *Globicephala melas*; **humpback**, *Megaptera novaeangliae*; and **finback**, *Balaenoptera physalus*, whales have come ashore dead in past years, and right whales have been sighted offshore.

White-tailed deer

Pinnipeds—Seals, sea lions and walruses. Pinnipeds are marine mammals that come ashore to breed, give birth and nurse their young. In island waters, only seals represent this group.

Seals. Two species of seals may be seen in the winter months around the Island: **harbor seal**, *Phoca vitulina*, and **gray seal**, *Halichoerus grypus*. The gray seal breeds in winter, and a large population can be found on Muskeget Island. They are often seen on the rocks at Squibnocket and other south shore beaches in winter.

Harbor seal

NEED MORE INFORMATION?

Here are some good general-resource books for Martha's Vineyard and New England plants and animals.

Cohen, Russ, *Wild Plants I Have Known and Eaten* (Essex County Greenbelt Association, 2004).

Holland, Mary, *Naturally Curious: A Photographic Field Guide and Month-by-Month Journey through the Fields, Woods, and Marshes of New England* (Trafalgar Square Books, 2010).

Keith, Allan R., Stephen A. Spongberg, *Island Life: A Catalog of the Biodiversity on and around Martha's Vineyard* (Allan Keith and the Marine Biological Laboratories, 2008).

Lee, Lindsey, *Edible Wild Plants of Martha's Vineyard* (Vineyard Conservation Society, 1999).

Martha's Vineyard Sandplain Restoration Project, *The Flora of Martha's Vineyard* (Mary P. Wakeman Conservation Center, n.d.).

Acknowledgments

The original *Moraine to Marsh* just might have been responsible for bringing me to the Island permanently. I spent a weekend in my parents' summer home in West Tisbury in 1999, reading the book cover to cover to learn as much as I could about the natural world of Martha's Vineyard. I wanted a job with The Trustees of Reservations teaching children and adults about the Island's natural resources, and *Moraine to Marsh* provided me with the background and knowledge I needed to prepare me for the interview and subsequently the job.

I had grown up in suburban New Jersey, and my parents had purchased a seasonal Island home after I graduated from college. I hadn't spent much time on the Vineyard, but it was a great job in a beautiful place that intrigued me.

Fourteen years later, now the director at Felix Neck Wildlife Sanctuary and nature writer for the *Vineyard Gazette*, my love of nature and the drive to share it guides this project and the life I have created here. *Moraine to Marsh* has always remained a favorite, but it went out of print after its 1988 printing, and the Island's remaining copies of the book slowly declined.

The ultimate goal of updating and bringing back this book is to continue the tradition of the original author, Anne Hale, of teaching and learning about the nature of Martha's Vineyard. Beyond fostering a love of place, the update and rewrite of this book directly supports the education and conservation work of Mass Audubon's Felix Neck Wildlife Sanctuary.

Anne Hale was one of the founders of the Felix Neck Wildlife Sanctuary and started Fern and Feather Camp at Felix Neck in 1964. This summer camp has become an Island tradition for many families, some with multiple generations attending. This year, 2014, marks 50 years of the camp, and the return of this rewritten classic honors the anniversary. Through Mass Audubon and with the help of donors that underwrote the costs of publication, the sale of this book will also financially support Felix Neck's education programs in the schools and community.

Anne Hale

Anne Hale had the vision, drive, and commitment to create the original book. Her family supported her, and the entire Hale family has supported me in this endeavor by donating the copyright and encouraging Felix Neck's efforts.

In the original book, Anne Hale relied on a cadre of Island naturalists, scientists, artists and photographers, friends, writers, and conservation professionals. Her list reads like a historical who's who of Vineyard natural history. These experts created the foundations on which we've built.

The idea to bring this book back to Vineyard audiences was hatched with Rob Kendall at a holiday party. He became the project's first donor and continued to cheer me on during the process.

Securing the financing to produce this book was pivotal in assuring that the sale of each book would raise funds for Felix Neck. Donations of all amounts made this book possible, but the financial commitment of the following individuals, foundations, and businesses must be acknowledged: Philip and Deborah Hale and the Hale families; the Ann E. Clark Private Foundation; Steve Allen; Robert and Patty Kendall; Henry P. Davis; the Felix Neck Wildlife Trust; the Martha's Vineyard Savings Bank; and John and Sharon Pearson, whose donation was given in memory of Dr. Bruce and Geraldine Harrold and Kathy Pearson; plus many other donors.

The Island's conservation lands are managed by many groups, each of which has its own mission, management, and goals. The properties highlighted include lands owned by the Martha's Vineyard Land Bank Commission, Mass Audubon, Sheriff's Meadow Foundation, the Commonwealth of Massachusetts (Department of Conservation and Recreation), the Wampanoag Tribe of Gay Head / Aquinnah, and The Trustees of Reservations. Thanks are extended to these groups for protecting and sharing some of the Island's most beautiful places.

Countless hours went into this project, and many who gave their time are volunteers. Emma Grace Ward got the project rolling by scanning and digitizing all of the original text. Members of the Felix Neck Sanctuary Committee and Felix Neck volunteers—including Penny Uhlendorf, Robert Culbert, Ellen Miller, Steve Auerbach, Janet Holladay, Andrea Hartman, Vasha Brunelle, Bill Bridwell, Oscar Thompson, Dave Nash, Robin Bray, Megan Ottens Sargent, David Hobart, and many others—provided assistance and support for the project. Current and former Mass Audubon staff—including Marion Hammond, Philip Hunsaker, Cristina Pereira, Laura Caruso, Josey Kirkland, Susie Bowman, Cathy Minkiewicz, Kathy Sferra,

Banks Poor, Gary Clayton, and Tara Henrichon—all played a part in the book's production. Staff of the Island's conservation organizations—including Kristin Fauteux, Julie Russell, John Varkonda, Chris Kennedy, Chris Seidel, and their colleagues—provided their time and talent and must be mentioned.

Steve Allen was there from the beginning, providing proofreading, editing, advice, and assistance through the entire process. Ellen Miller and Bob Mill offered their editing expertise, as did Jan Pogue, making each version stronger.

Tim Johnson spent many days walking the trails and capturing the photographs that give this book its beauty. Other photographers who contributed their work include Dave Nash, Nathalie Woodruff, Judy Holland McChesney, Penny Uhlendorf, Steve Auerbach, Bill Brine, Justen Walker, Susie Schwoch, Grace Burton Sundman, and Alex Cohen.

We are fortunate to have the original drawings by Marcia Wise. Even after 25 years, she was able to locate the originals and shared them generously with us. Dana Gaines helped us fill in the gaps, creating maps that speak to the Vineyard's charm and spirit.

Jan Pogue of Vineyard Stories published this book and provided gentle guidance, encouragement, and expertise—plus everything else needed to make a good book. Her late husband, John Walter, must also be mentioned. Though he died in 2008 he hired me to write for the *Vineyard Gazette*, seeing a talent that I didn't know I had and showing me a new way to reach out and share Island nature.

My family and friends rallied behind me, especially my husband, Jean-Marc Dupon, who fed me love, support, and the occasional crème brûlée to keep me going and manage the stress that came from producing a book the same year that we planned and executed our wedding.

This book, Anne Hale's labor of love, has become my own. Our mutual passion for nature and sharing it with others drove both of us to this same point—25 years apart, yet at this moment coming together to continue the work that was started so many years ago. To study, teach, and appreciate nature—a vital calling and important endeavor.

The changes that have come over the years in the natural world are a reason to cheer and a reason to fear. But most of all, knowledge brings care and protection. In this time of new threats, including climate change and sea-level rise, only an educated and inspired community can achieve stewardship and safeguard the Island's unique nature.

Suzan Bellincampi
February, 2014

Glossary

Amphibian: Cold-blooded vertebrate of the class Amphibia. These land animals generally breed in water and include frogs, salamanders, toads, and others.

Anuran: An amphibian of the order Anura that includes frogs and toads.

Arachnid: A member of the class Arachnida, which includes spiders, mites, ticks, and others. These insects are invertebrates and have four pairs of jointed legs and a two-part body.

Arthropod: An invertebrate member of the phylum Arthropoda. Insects, crustaceans, and arachnids, among others, are included in this phylum and are characterized by their exoskeleton and segmented body.

Barrier beach: An elongated sand deposit built by littoral currents and waves generally parallel to the shore, whose crest rises above high water.

Biome (biotic community): Association of interrelated and interdependent life-forms.

Bog: A type of wetland with spongy acidic soils often composed of sphagnum moss and peat.

Boreal: Growing in northern and mountainous areas of the northern hemisphere.

Bottoms (frost bottoms): Low areas formed by southward-flowing meltwater streams from the Wisconsin glacier.

Brackish: Waters that are a mixture of fresh and salt water. Coastal marshes and estuaries generally contain brackish or moderately salty water.

Buzzards Bay lobe: The glacial ice lobe of the Wisconsin glaciations that moved from southern Massachusetts and northern Rhode Island and built the western section of the Martha's Vineyard moraine, which formed most Up-Island terrain.

Cape Cod lobe: The lobe of the Wisconsin glaciers that moved southeast across Cape Cod Bay and built the eastern section of the moraine, which forms most of Down-Island and is mostly overlain by outwash from the Buzzards Bay lobe.

Cenozoic: The current era of geological time, beginning after the Cretaceous extinction about 65 million years ago.

Cetacean: A marine mammal from the order Cetacea that includes whales, porpoises, and dolphins.

Climax vegetation (woodland): The stage in succession when a relatively stable stage is reached and persists because it does not create conditions that are unfavorable to itself or that favor invasion of better-adapted forms.

Coastal plain: A low seaboard plain that represented sea floor during a former time of higher sea level.

Community: A group of interdependent and interrelated plants and animals.

Continental drift: Movement of tectonic plates of the earth's crust.

Continental shelf: The flat, gently sloping edge of the continent, now mostly covered by shallow seawaters.

Consumer: Any living thing that is unable to manufacture food from nonliving substances and depends instead on the energy stored in other living things.

Cretaceous: The period of the Mesozoic era from 140 million years ago to 65 million years ago. It is characterized by the development of flowering plants and mammals, and the extinction of many earlier life-forms, such as dinosaurs.

Crustaceans: The large class of animals that includes crabs, lobsters, and shrimp. Crustaceans typically live in water and are characterized by jointed legs, segmented bodies, and hard external skeletons.

Decomposers: Living plants and animals, chiefly fungi and bacteria, that exist by extracting energy from decaying tissues of dead plants and animals. In the process they release simple chemical compounds stored in the dead bodies and make them available once again for use by green plants.

Detritus: Particles of the decaying remains of dead plants and animals, an important source of food for many marsh animals.

Down-Island: The eastern end of the Island; the term derives from a sailing term that means sailing in the direction of the prevailing southwesterly wind of summer, downwind or toward the east.

Drift: Any sort of glacial deposit.

Echinoderm: Marine invertebrates from the phylum Echinodermata that are characterized by a hard, spiny covering or skin, and include sea stars, sea cucumbers, and sea urchins.

Ecology: The science of the interrelationships of all living things to each other and their environment.

Ecosystem: A complex of a biotic community and its nonliving environment that contains the requirements for all life within the system and that interact to form a functioning whole.

Environment: All the external conditions, such as soil, water, air, and organisms, surrounding a living thing.

Erratic: A glacially transported boulder.

Estuary: The portion of a river or bay affected by the rise and fall of the tide that contains a mixture of fresh and salt water.

Fault: A fracture in the earth's crust accompanied by a displacement of one side of the fracture with respect to the other.

Filter feeders: Animals such as clams and mussels that obtain food by filtering or straining it from surrounding waters.

Flood tide: An unusually high tide often caused by a combination of factors such as storms or a particular alignment of the sun, moon, and earth.

Fold: A bend in rock created by lateral compression.

Food chain: The passage of energy and materials in the form of food from producers (green plants) through a succession of plant-eating and meat-eating consumers.

Food web: A system of interlocking food chains. Since few animals rely on a single food source and since a given food is rarely consumed exclusively by a single species of animals, the separate food chains in any natural community interlock and form a web.

Frost bottom: See *Bottoms*.

Glacial drift: Sediments accumulated as a result of glaciation, under a glacier, at its margins or beyond.

Glacial till: An unsorted and unstratified sediment deposited directly by a glacier in moraines and not reworked by meltwater.

Great pond: A pond of 10 acres of more.

Greensand: A sandy deposit consisting mainly of the green mineral glauconite.

Groundwater: Water found in pore spaces and cracks within earth's upper crust.

Gulf Stream: A major north-south current system that brings warm water up along the East Coast from the Gulf of Mexico.

Habitat: A place where a plant or animal is characteristically found.

Hardwoods: Nonconiferous trees.

Hydroids: Members of the class Hydrozoa that are aquatic animals with an internal body cavity living in colonies.

Interglacial stage: A major interval within the Pleistocene Epoch, separating successive glacial stages.

Intertidal zone (littoral zone): Generally considered to be the zone between mean high-water and mean low-water levels.

Invertebrate: An animal without a backbone, such as insects and mollusks.

Illinoian: A period of geologic time that occurred approximately 300,000 to 130,000 years ago during the Pleistocene epoch.

Jurassic: A period of geologic time that occurred approximately 199.6 million to 145.5 million years ago.

Kettle holes: Depressions left by melting glacial ice blocks that had broken off the face of a glacier. Bogs often form in these depressions.

Labrador current: A surface ocean current that passes around Newfoundland and along the coast and intersects with the Gulf stream.

Larva: An active immature stage in an animal's life history, during which its form differs from that of the adult. The caterpillar, for example, is the larva of a butterfly; the tadpole is the larval stage in the life history of a frog.

Laurussia: A former landmass composed of Asia, North America, and other minor land masses of the northern hemisphere.

Lignite: A very low-grade coal that often contains plant matter.

Littoral current: A current moving parallel to the shore, usually developed by wave fronts that have an angular approach to the shore.

Lowlands: Land whose surface is relatively close to the water table.

Marsh: A treeless form of wetland, often developing in shallow ponds or depressions, tidal areas and estuaries. Marshes may contain either salt or fresh water. Grasses and sedges are prominent forms of vegetation.

Meltwater stream: Water flows created by the melting and flowing of water from a glacier.

Mesozoic: The era of geological time from 250 million years ago to 65 million years ago, including the Triassic, Jurassic, and Cretaceous periods.

Miocene: Epoch in the Cenozoic era, Tertiary period, from 23 million to 5 million years ago, when large amounts of marine deposits were laid down on the coastal plain.

Mollusks: A major group of animals with soft, boneless bodies and, usually, shells. The group includes snails, clams, mussels, scallops, and oysters.

Martha's Vineyard moraine: Terminal moraine of the Island, which includes deposits from the Buzzards Bay and Cape Cod ice lobes.

Moraine, recessional: Glacial deposits left when the ice paused in its retreat.

Moraine, terminal: A deposit left by a glacier at its terminus, forming a ridge that marks the farthest limits of the glacier.

Orogeny: The folding and faulting of the earth's crust that results in the formation of mountains and other geological features.

Outwash: Deposits of sand and gravel carried from glacial ice, sorted and spread by meltwater streams to form a delta-like plain.

Paleozoic: The geological era that occurred between 570 million and 230 million years ago, during which fish, insects, and reptiles appeared.

Pangaea: A continent that formed in the Paleozoic era through a process of continental drift and comprised all the separate continents of the world.

Panthalassa Sea: The universal sea that surrounded Pangaea.

Peat: Partly decayed organic matter formed in boggy areas where high acidity and a lack of oxygen limit decomposition.

Pelagic: Living in the open sea.

Photosynthesis: The process by which green plants convert carbon dioxide and water into simple sugars. Chlorophyll and sunlight are essential to the series of complex chemical reactions involved.

Pinniped: The group of marine mammals that includes seals, sea lions, and walruses.

Pioneer plants: Plants that grow on bare soil or rock.

Plankton: The plants and animals that float or swim weakly near the surface of a body of water. These are often minute and are an important food source for many aquatic animals.

Pleistocene: That epoch in the earth's history from about 2.6 million to 12,000 years ago that is characterized by widespread glaciations.

Producers: Green plants, which are the basic link in any food chain, that manufacture their own food via photosynthesis.

Quartz: A mineral form of silica, widely distributed in rocks.

Red tide (harmful algal bloom [HAB]): A red or reddish-brown discoloration of surface waters most frequently occurring in coastal regions and caused by concentrations of certain microscopic organisms that produce toxic substances. When ingested by filter-feeding shellfish, the algae can make the shellfish unfit for human consumption.

Rush: A kind of plant resembling grasses that tends to grow in cool, wet areas.

Salinity: A measure of the quantity of dissolved salts in sea water.

Salt marsh: A tidally influenced saltwater wetland characterized by the presence of grasses, sedges, and other salt-friendly plants.

Sedge: A kind of plant resembling the grasses. However, sedges usually have solid triangular stems in contrast to the round stems of grasses and rushes.

Seral stage: A stage, or series of ecological communities—seres—that succeed one another in the biotic development of an area or formation.

Sori: Spore cases on the underside of the fronds (leaves) of ferns.

Stratification: The arrangement of sedimentary rocks in beds or strata in an undisturbed sequence, the older at the bottom.

Succession: The gradual displacement of one biotic community by another, eventually leading to a more stable climax community.

Swamp: A form of wetland characterized by mosses, shrubs, and trees such as red maples and beetlebungs. Swamps usually have better drainage than bogs.

Tectonic plates: Slabs of solid rock—segments of the earth's crust—that slowly move, causing geologic landscape change.

Tertiary: That period in earth history characterized by the dominance of mammals.

Thrust plain: A nearly horizontal geological fault.

Up-Island: Designation for the western part of the Island. Derived from sailing terminology to sail upwind against the prevailing southwesterlies of summer.

Ventifact: A smooth, faceted rock, pitted and frosted by the bombardment of windborne sand formed on the Vineyard during periods of glaciation.

Vertebrate: An animal with a backbone. The group includes fishes, amphibians, reptiles, birds, and mammals.

Water table: The upper level of the underground reservoir of water.

Wisconsin glacier: The final glacial stage within the Pleistocene epoch. Most of the visible ice deposits of the Vineyard arrived in the Wisconsin glaciation.

Wrack line: Line where high tides leave flotsam and jetsam from the ocean.

INDEX